# The
# Parent
# Project

# The Parent Project

## A Workshop Approach to Parent Involvement

James Vopat

*Carroll College, Waukesha, WI*
*Director, Milwaukee Writing Project*

Stenhouse Publishers
Portland, Maine

Stenhouse Publishers

**Library of Congress Cataloging-in-Publication Data**
Vopat, James
     The parent project : a workshop approach to parent involvement /
James Vopat.
        p.   cm.
     Includes bibliographical references.
     ISBN 1-57110-001-6
     1. Education—Parent participation—Wisconsin—Milwaukee.
     I. Title.
LC225.32.W62M558    1994                        94-20935
370.19'31—dc20                                  CIP


ISBN 1-57110-001-6

The author and publisher would like to thank the following for permission to reprint previously published material:

*Page 24:* "Surviving (and Enjoying) Workshop #1" by Robbie McLoud. Originally published in *Growing with La Escuela Fratney: Year II.* Reprinted by permission.

*Fig. 15, page 88:* "101 Ways to Praise a Child" reprinted by permission of Charter Hospital of Milwaukee.

*Page 171:* "Multicultural Bibliography of Children's Books" prepared by Book Bay, Milwaukee, Wisconsin. Reprinted by permission.

*Page 181:* "Parent Resources" bibliography. Reprinted from Vol. 8 Number 3, *Rethinking Schools,* 1001 E. Keefe Ave., Milwaukee, WI 53212. 414-964-9646.


Logo art by Ajala Heighes and art on page 61 by Brian Clark.


Back-cover photo by Sandra Zinos
Cover and interior design by Maria Szmauz
Editorial and production services by Nancy Sheridan
Typeset by Octal Publishing, Inc., Salem, NH

Manufactured in the United States of America on acid-free paper
05                 9 8 7 6

*T*his book is dedicated to the foundations that have supported development of the Parent Project: The Faye McBeath Foundation, The Milwaukee Foundation, and especially The Joyce Foundation of Chicago.

# Contents

AUTHOR'S NOTE • ix

ACKNOWLEDGMENTS • xi

AN INTRODUCTION TO THE PARENT
PROJECT • 1

OUR PHILOSOPHY FOR THE PARENT
PROJECT • 7

HOW TO BEGIN THE PARENT PROJECT • 13
Details   15

WORKSHOP STRUCTURE AND
AMBIANCE • 21
Running a Parent Workshop: A Sample Schedule   22
Like the Ambiance? Factors Conducive to a Successful
Workshop   27

JOURNALS • 35

CIRCLE OF BELIEF • 43

BEYOND WORKSHOP 1: A THREE-YEAR
PLAN • 49
*I May Not Know What I'm Doing This Afternoon, But I Have a
Three-Year Plan* 50
*Follow-Up* 51
*Leadership Institute* 53

WORKSHOPS ANYONE? • 57
*Introductory Community-Building Workshop* 58
*Reading Workshops* 62
*Writing Workshops* 69
*Self-Esteem Workshops* 78
*Special-Interest Workshops* 90
*Closure/Celebration Workshop* 97
*Resources: All of Us* 99

PUBLICATION • 103

EVALUATION • 111
*But, Does It Work?* 113
*The Hi-Mount Study* 115

ADVOCACY • 119

FREQUENTLY ASKED QUESTIONS ABOUT THE
PARENT PROJECT • 125

RESOURCES

ORGANIZATION AND ADMINISTRATION • 135

WORKSHOP MATERIALS • 145

READ ON—THE BEST ENDINGS ARE
BEGINNINGS • 161

WORKS CITED • 191

# Author's Note

This book tells the story of the Parent Project and provides materials that will help you start and maintain a program of your own. The workshop approach as a way to achieve parent involvement is explained in the first chapters. Then a detailed description of sixteen workshops I have found to be especially effective follows. You are invited to adapt and refine these workshops in whatever ways you find helpful and, of course, to develop your own.

Since it is my intent to honor the voice of workshop participants—parents, children, and teachers—their writing is presented as it was received with no further editing. The children's artwork in this book was in response to parent writing and originally appeared in project publications (see "Publication," p. 103).

# Acknowledgments

To Mary Rose O'Reilley, who set so much in motion;

To Joan Yuen, who was willing to give 110%, and did;

To Dave Gawlik, who made things visible;

To Spence Korte, who opened the doors and kept them open;

To Marian Catania, Bertha Zamudio, Becky Trayser, Robbie McLoud, Mercedes Riviera, Katherine Dummer, Mary Foskett, Bonnie Robinson, Angela Hudson, and all the parents and teachers;

To Philippa Stratton and Tom Seavey for their spirit of adventure;

To Nancy Sheridan for her good judgment;

To Smokey and Elaine—

This wouldn't exist without all of you.

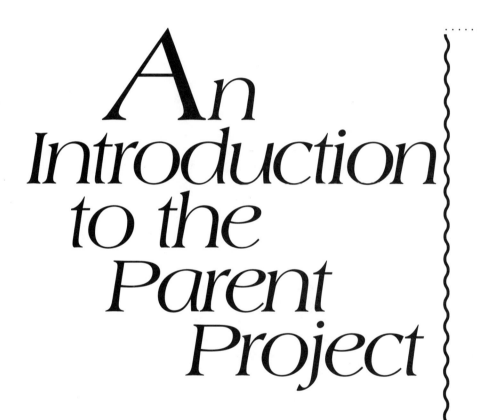

# An Introduction to the Parent Project

WELCOME to the Parent Project. The Project is a workshop approach to increasing parent involvement in their children's education. The Parent Project began six years ago in three of Milwaukee's inner-city elementary schools in response to a specific practical need. As Director of the Milwaukee Writing Project, I was at the time working with Milwaukee teachers in an effort to revitalize classroom instruction through the use of journals, portfolios, and workshop structures. Concerns regarding parent understanding and support for the kinds of instructional changes teachers were making arose with such regularity that I began to search for a means for involving parents in the process.

Fortuitously, The Joyce Foundation of Chicago was, during this same period, determined to support a variety of efforts to increase parent involvement in their children's education. Since there didn't seem to be any available model for the kind of parent involvement I envisioned, The Joyce Foundation encouraged me to work with Milwaukee teachers and parents in order to develop such a program. What emerged was a workshop approach that focused on what children were learning in the classroom, and how this learning could be supported at home. What emerged was a means to strengthen the relationship between home and school—teacher, parent, and child.

School has changed dramatically since many parents were there and, if the goal of parent involvement is to strengthen the link between home and school, parents need to be introduced to the revitalized school classroom. Many classroom learning strategies experienced by children every day—keeping journals, interviewing, book sharing, cooperative learning, response groups, publishing—are unfamiliar to these same children's parents. We can't really expect parents to nurture and support such learning strategies if they don't understand what those strategies are or how they can be supported.

For example, in one of our initial parent workshops, I invited everyone to write or draw for five minutes in their journals. After we were finished, I asked for comments. Wayne said he knew he had misspelled many words and that he never could spell and it bothered him. We talked about how journal writing didn't need to be correct and that the freedom simply to express one's self was one of the advantages of keeping a journal. Wayne's two daughters (in grades one and three) were keeping journals in school, and Wayne said that when they brought their journals home, the first thing on his mind when he read them was how they were doing on their spelling.

When Wayne was in elementary school, there was no journal writing and good writing meant spelling correctly and nothing more. For Wayne's two daughters, writing in school had come to be defined so differently that, for them, the messages of school and home were contradictory. As I listened to Wayne joke about his spelling and admit his relief at not having to worry about it when using his journal, I thought about how absurd it is to reform education but then to keep it a secret from parents.

The counterargument often heard is not that school reform is a kept secret but that parents just won't show up to hear about it. I have a few observations about this. First of all, I am curious as to what happens when the parent does show up and what kind of support structure is in place for follow-up. In Milwaukee, for instance, it has been popular to bring busloads of parents into large auditoriums for info-motivational seminars where they are blamed, tantalized, and talked at. At the end of the day, these parents are bussed home where they have to deal with the everyday problems that have accumulated. And that's it. There is no follow-up support, only a slightly bitter tomorrow.

Instead of this lack of support, what would happen if we called upon the most powerful aspects of school reform to accomplish the goal of increased parent involvement: workshops, journals, cooperative groups, shared reading, agenda building, interviewing, goal setting, and critical thinking?

What would happen? Through our workshops, we have spent years exploring the answers to this question, working with thousands of parents and teachers in a wide range of settings, including inner-city schools, community centers, affluent and not-so-affluent suburban schools, as well as Chapter 1 programs. So what did happen?

When I meet with parents and teachers in order to discuss parent involvement and define the advantages of a workshop approach, I usually begin by conducting a workshop itself as a means of coming to understand by doing rather than talking about doing. After a brief introduction of all participants and an explanation of why we are together, I distribute journals. I explain that the journals should be used in ways participants find comfortable—writing, drawing, doodling—whatever will help them remember what they feel is important. I then ask everyone to pause a moment, relax, and think back to when they were growing up. What influence did their parents or guardians have on their attitudes and feelings about school and learning?

Did your parents or care-giver actively encourage you to learn, were they neutral, or did they discourage learning? Does one particular incident from the past come to mind? Can you place yourself back in this memory? Can you close your eyes for a few minutes and try to reexperience this memory, this time and place? Can you close your eyes and go back, into this time and place? [long pause]

Journey back into this memory, Where are you? How old are you? Who's with you? How do you feel? What's happening? Have your feelings about this memory changed over time? Why do you think this memory has stayed with you? What are the dimensions of its meaning? [long pause]

Now, if you will open your eyes and take a few minutes to jot down some reactions to this visualization of your memory. Any words or pictures or part of images that come to mind. Anything that will help you remember it.

What does your memory have to say about the connection between parents, schools, and learning?

What can we do to increase parents' involvement in their children's education?

After there has been sufficient time for reflection, I divide participants into small groups of four or five people and ask them to share their individual memory with the other members of their group by reading from their journal or verbally recounting what they have been thinking about. When everyone has had an opportunity to share, I ask each group to formulate some observations about what constitutes a positive home environment for learning and to arrive at these observations based on the memories of their group.

When the small groups report back to the reformed large group, they usually do so with a combination of moving family history and reasonable, clear educational philosophy. As we hear these family stories and the resulting observations about how learning can be fostered and nurtured, the significance of parent involvement becomes all the more real. As we listen to the family stories of sacrifice for education; of persistence in school in spite of daunting obstacles; of parents reading to their children, writing with their children, encouraging learning as a sign of self-worth, it becomes obvious that the issue is not whether parent involvement is necessary, but rather how we can all work together to make it more intentional.

*Cynthia Williams/Kenyetta Williams*

I HAVE MEMORIES OF . . . . . . .
YOU AS MY FAT BABY, TOO BIG FOR ME TO CARRY
YOU WHEN YOU TOOK YOUR FIRST STEPS, I WAS SO HAPPY
YOU AND YOUR FIRST BIRTHDAY PARTY, JUST YOU AND ME
YOU AT YOUR FIRST DAY OF SCHOOL, YOU WERE EXCITED ABOUT IT
YOU AND YOUR BROTHER SPENDING THE SUMMER TOGETHER, YOU
GUYS HAD FUN
YOU AND YOUR FIRST PAIR OF GLASSES, YOU LOOK JUST LIKE ME
YOU LOSING YOUR FIRST TOOTH AND GOT A WHOLE DOLLAR FOR IT
YOUR FIRST TRIP TO CHICAGO ON THE GREYHOUND BUS, WE HAD FUN
YOU RIDING YOUR BIKE THAT ONLY TOOK YOU TWENTY MINUTES TO
LEARN HOW TO RIDE
YOUR FIRST OVERNITE STAY AT CAMP, AND HOW YOU WANTED TO
STAY LONGER
HOW YOU LOVE TO SWIM AND PLAY IN WATER
BUT MOST OF ALL
            I HAVE MEMORIES OF HOW MUCH WE LOVE EACH OTHER

TO KENYETTA
            WITH ALL MY LOVE
                        YOUR MOTHER CYNTHIA

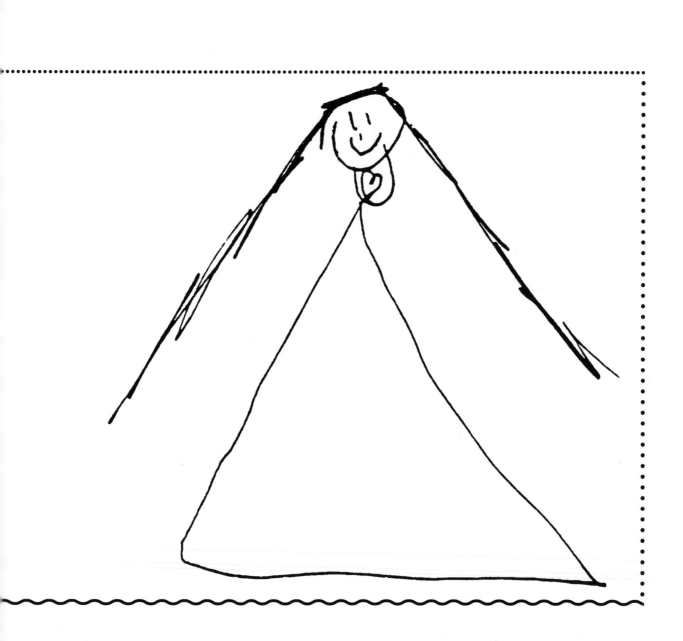

*Our
Philosophy
for the
Parent
Project*

In 1991, The Joyce Foundation, which had supported development of the Parent Project, asked for a brief description of the program philosophy. Still in the midst of understanding what the Parent Project would mean, I submitted the following:

True school reform can only be accomplished through the understanding, support, and commitment of parents. The dilemma is that many parents feel disaffected from school, many aren't sure how they can best help their child succeed, and many have no support and encouragement for their own accomplishments as "parents."

One way to unite the twin goals of school reform and parent advocacy is to establish learning collaborations among parents, their children, and their children's teachers. When such collaborations involve positive experiences with the content of a renewed school curriculum, then an ongoing partnership between parent, teacher, and child/student is established through the values of learning. For those parents who have negative feelings about school and/or teachers, such a collaboration redefines the promise and worth of education.

Parents can best help their children succeed in school when they themselves have had positive experiences with writing, reading, and learning. Parents can best help their children succeed in school when they know how to foster and connect the learning in the home environment with the learning in school. Rather than viewing parents, teachers, school, and home as distinct and separate, we need to honor the primary relationship they all have in common: learning and how to insure its success.

Now, the five-year "pilot project" of the Parent Project completed, the philosophy seems a lot simpler: instead of blaming and complaining about parents, we need to give them access. And not just parents, but teachers too. The following anonymous writing was left by a teacher after an open forum for Milwaukee teachers on the subject of parent involvement:

Many of the parents of the kids at Story are caring and loving and concerned for their children. They want more for their kids than they've had. They just don't know how to go about it or if they do, there is the eternal time crunch about when they can give the time they know they should be giving. Many of them are single, working parents. Their priorities are earning power and money to provide the basics for their kids. They don't come to school, open houses, conferences. You can't get hold of them even on the phone many times. I feel alone with their kids, their kids' problems. I get frustrated because I can't solve the problems alone.

They key word here is *alone*. The key word in the Parent Project is *together*.

Teachers, I have found, certainly have as much to gain from the workshops as parents. For teachers, the workshops enlarge the learning as well as human context of the children they teach. Working with parents bridges the often formidable, formal, hands-off chasm that exists between home and school. Just as workshops help demystify school and teachers for parents, so they help demystify parents for teachers. "Working together" sounds great but is really only feasible when those who are expected to be "together" know and feel comfortable with each other. In addition, because of their experiential nature, our workshops give parents and teachers a chance to accomplish things as equal partners. For, after all, as has been frequently said, the parent is the child's first teacher.

Such working partnerships between parents and teachers provide an added benefit to the school itself. Teachers and parents need each other as advocates for authentic learning—not only in the classroom and the home, but also before the School Board, on the School Board, at public forums, and in private deliberations. Through Parent Project workshops, "them" rather quickly becomes "us."

Cecilia Vallejo/Carrie Vallejo

*CARRIE*
*CARINOSA Y SUAVE*
*JUGANDO, DIBUJANDO, LEYENDO*
*ERES TAN AMOROSA*
*CARRIE*

CARRIE
AFFECTIONATE AND SOFT
PLAYING, DRAWING, READING
YOU ARE SO LOVING
CARRIE

# How to Begin the Parent Project

When people ask how our Parent Project operates, I often respond that what we have to offer is a structure that promotes increased parent involvement in their children's education, not a parenting curriculum. When I speak of a "workshop" approach to parent involvement, I am describing a process rather than a product, the means to an end, a group dynamic rather than a predetermined outcome.

For us, "workshop" means a group of parents, teachers, and school support staff working together for the betterment of children and families. The composition of the workshop group varies, but we strive for fifteen to twenty parents, two or three teachers, the school social worker or psychologist, and two co-facilitators. Workshop participants set their own agendas, rely on the group as a resource, and reach into their individual and collective experiences as a source of strength and problem solving.

Each parent workshop generally lasts two hours and includes a mix of experiential activities, guest presentations, journal writing, shared books, and specific attention to what parents can do at home to support what their children are learning in school. Our workshops are successful because:

- we do things instead of talking about doing them;
- we see teachers and parents as equals;
- we advocate for children.

We have tried to keep our structure and delivery simple. Basically, we begin by offering the group a series of six weekly two-hour workshops. At the end of the six weeks, parents and teachers are invited to continue to participate through monthly follow-up workshops. We then begin another six-week group whose members will eventually join the follow-up network.

This is an ongoing process and clearly needs commitment from the school community: teachers, administrators, staff, parents, and students. Along with this commitment comes the crucial sense of control, responsibility, and ownership of the Project by the individual school community it serves. But before the first formal workshop, before the parent and teacher participants can be identified, definition and discussion of parent involvement needs to occur among everyone in the school community. Sometimes reaching all constituencies is difficult—sometimes impossible—which is all the more reason to generate a Parent Project.

Once there is a consensus that increased parent involvement is a priority, the workshop facilitators need to be identified. Teachers who are already accustomed to running their own process classrooms, which include reading and writing workshops, are natural choices to become Project co-facilitators. Co-facilitators can also be trained (see "Leadership Institute," p. 53). Ideally, co-facilitators are a team of teachers and parents, although in the initial stages in many schools, the co-facilitators are teachers. In some sites, parent aids make fine co-facilitators since they are already providing the connections between home and school.

Identification of the parent participants can be handled in a number of ways. Some schools have the teachers personally contact the parents to explain the benefits of the program and how specifically it will help their children. Other schools send out large mailings and reserve space on a first-come, first-served basis. If parents want to participate in a program, but it is full, it is important to be able to offer them space in another workshop in the not-too-distant future.

Of course, there has to be an individual or a group of individuals who start this adventure, and while identification of participants and the nature of the workshop are paramount, there are suddenly many other details and questions to consider.

## DETAILS

## IDENTIFICATION OF PARTICIPANTS

Workshop size can vary, but when the number of participants exceeds twenty-five, it is a good idea to split the large group into smaller groups for sharing and discussion. The smaller groups can then report to the larger group for closure and continuity. In general, we try to identify a minimum of fifteen parents and two teachers to participate in the initial six-week workshop series. Since many discussions revolve around child development and behavior issues, we have found that it is beneficial also to include the school social worker or staff psychologist in group meetings. Participating parents are identified by the school—either through direct teacher contact, an informational meeting, or home mailing. An optimum time to approach parents about the benefits of participation in the workshops is during parent/teacher conferences.

## TIME

The actual meeting time of the workshops varies with the school or agency. Workshop sessions generally last two hours. Some schools find parents prefer to meet directly after the formal school day ends (say from 4:00 P.M. to 6:00 P.M.), while others find that parents prefer to meet after dinner (6:30 P.M. to 8:30 P.M.). Whatever the time slot, it is important that the day of the meeting be consistent from week to week.

## PLACE

A stimulating, comfortable schoolroom or library is a conducive place to hold the workshops. The room should be able to accommodate participants' movement between small and large groups and needs to have seating that can be arranged in a circle. *No sitting in rows*. While there are great advantages to holding the workshops in a school classroom, workshops should never be conducted in a way that treats parents like students or makes them feel like they have been sent back to grade school. The purpose of holding the workshops in a classroom is to give parents access to their children's imaginative creativity, which should be apparent in various projects and artwork displayed around the room.

## CHILD CARE

We provide on-site child care for children of all participants, including teachers. We make every effort to ensure that the child care is more than baby-sitting. In ideal situations, child care involves the children in constructive, fun learning activities that complement the focus of the parent workshops. At some school sites, child care is already in place for other after-school programs and can be used by workshop participants. At other sites, we have been able to coordinate arrangements with the school district's after-school recreation program. In assembling a child-care staff, we have found it helpful to contact local high schools for names of students with suitable child-care experience.

## TRANSPORTATION

Naturally, the workshops cannot occur if the parents are unable to get there. We try to arrange car pools, and when this fails, we budget funds for transportation (usually by taxi).

## STIPENDS AND OTHER INCENTIVES
## FOR PARTICIPATION

Whenever possible, we provide stipends for all participants, including parents, teachers, and the school social worker. Funds for stipends come from grants or the school budget. Stipends for parents are currently one hundred dollars for a six-week workshop series (or approximately eight dollars per hour). Stipends for teachers and the social worker are usually at their hourly rate. Parent stipends are for each participant—not per family. Some individuals may object to the parent stipend. These same individuals, however, may also insist on being paid for their time. What needs to be understood is that parent involvement does cost parents money. In addition to the workshop meetings, we encourage parents to visit their children's classrooms, involve themselves in appropriate ways in these classrooms, participate in school governance, and pursue their own educational goals. Such involvement invariably costs money (child-care costs, transportation, tuition for continuing education courses), and we feel obligated to do everything we can to make such involvement economically feasible. In affluent school districts the stipends for parents do not seem to be as significant a factor as in impoverished urban areas. While parents are informed of the stipend when they sign up for the Parent Project, we try to make sure that the stipend does not become the primary motivation for involvement. Stipends should not be seen as "paying parents to participate," but rather as a means to make their participation possible. We have a workshop sign-in sheet and generally pay the stipends (by money order) at the conclusion of the entire workshop series. Teacher stipends make it possible for teachers to give long-term commitment to the program.

## COMMITMENT FORM

We formalize the stipends, the child care, meeting times and place with a commitment form that parents sign before the start of the initial workshop (see page 137).

## JOURNALS

Participants' journals are the "glue" that provides continuity between workshop activities and meetings. We distribute journals to all participants when they attend their first workshop. At this time, we also show parents how to make journals at home for their children and invite teachers to share and discuss different kinds of journals from their classrooms (see "Journals," beginning on page 35).

## MULTILINGUAL WORKSHOPS
• • • • • • • • • • • • • • • • • • • • • • • • • • • • • • • • • • • • • • • • • • • • • • • • • • • • • • • •

Por Supuesto! Generally, teachers and parents can handle the translation between languages. It is important that the group reflects the cultural makeup of the school population. We are not in favor of separating parents into language groups. Our aim, instead, is to underline and support the school community. It takes a little more time to conduct multilingual workshops, but it is entirely worth it. The added benefit is that everyone also learns to appreciate different cultures and languages. Of course, to recruit parents to participate in multilingual workshops means that preliminary information and workshop materials need to be as user-friendly as possible and made available in the different languages of participants.

*Debbie Skinner/Terrance Porter*

TERRANCE
friendly, happy
playing, running, drawing,
likes to do everything (busy bee)
TERRANCE

# Workshop Structure and Ambiance

A workshop by definition has to be a certain duration; there must be enough time for concepts to be presented, worked with, and discussed. In our experience, parents and teachers respond more enthusiastically when they participate in activities than when they are told about them. There is a big difference between talking about journals and actually keeping one; between talking about reading books to children and actually opening the book and enjoying it.

We make every attempt to have our workshops reflect the kinds of learning taking place in the school classrooms. In this way, parents get a first-hand sense of the value of what their children are learning. Our workshops generally incorporate the following:

- journal writing
- shared reading of children's literature
- a guest presentation on a topic of group interest
- an experiential activity
- small and whole group discussion
- home application of workshop strategies

Because our agenda is participant-driven, it means that structure is organic and not content-specific. In other words, it is the recurrence of activities that gives us our sense of direction—indeed, our sense of possibilities. It is our hope that these same kinds of learning strategies also occur in the school. We are continually impressed by how quickly parents start to bring many of these same activities into their homes and make them their own.

## RUNNING A PARENT WORKSHOP: A SAMPLE SCHEDULE

As discussed in the previous chapter, we find it most productive to schedule two-hour workshops. This gives enough time to have some introductory follow-up from the last week's workshop, a guest presentation, and some meaningful application.

### WHO'S HERE, WHY ARE WE HERE, AND WHAT'S HAPPENED SINCE WE LAST MET? (30 minutes)

It is extremely important to "reform" the group every time it meets. For us, this usually involves a warm greeting, a preview of the evening's focus, and then a welcome round of introductions in which everyone introduces themselves, the names and ages of their children, and relates some comment or observation about the previous week's Parent Project activity. If we have extra time, we ask parents and teachers for any school "news" from the previous week.

## GUEST PRESENTATION (30 minutes)

Parents and teachers enjoy hearing from experts on topics immediately relevant to their own lives and their hopes (and fears) for their children: fire safety, lead poisoning, the new math, self-esteem, journal writing, scribble stories, child development. At best, the guest presentation fits into the evening's workshop focus and generates interactive discussion and/or a hands-on activity. We all sit around a circle together, and we encourage our guest to see themselves as a workshop participant as well. We discourage lecturing and try to see the guest presentation as having room for conversation and interaction. One memorable guest presentation, for example, involved a student teacher from the school showing the parents how they could use creative dramatics at home by actually doing six activities with them (see "FREEZE! It's a Creative Dramatics Workshop," page 94). There would have been universal disappointment if the student teacher had spent her entire time telling us about creative dramatics instead of letting us do them. We invite all guests to stay for the entire two hours of the workshop and to participate as fully as they can.

## BREAK (10 minutes)

The break is sometimes the most crucial Parent Project time. It allows for socializing as well as spontaneous small group discussions between parents and teachers. If the workshop takes place in the late afternoon, say 4:00 P.M. to 6:00 P.M., then we try to provide coffee, soda, and some real food (like sandwiches, pizza, or salad). If the workshop is held after dinnertime, say 6:30 P.M. to 8:30 P.M., then we try to provide coffee, soda, and some cookies.

## REGROUP AND DISCUSSION OF GUEST PRESENTATION (40 minutes)

At this point, we are interested in how parents and teachers individually respond to the guest presentation and how they can apply what they have observed to home and classroom. Usually we break into small groups of three or four and then report back and discuss in the large group towards the end. This is a good time for sharing children's books, writing in journals, and listening to classroom news from the teachers.

## ASSIGNMENT FOR NEXT WEEK, WRAP-UP, AND BOLT FOR THE DOOR (10 minutes)

Everyone needs to agree on some practical application of the evening's workshop to try out during the week at school or home: for example, "catching" your child doing something good after the self-esteem workshop; checking a book out of the library with your child after the library "field trip"; reading your story to your child and having him or her illustrate it with a self-portrait after the writing workshop. We will then begin the next week with our observations about how this activity has worked.

Whether the workshop ends at 4:30 P.M. or 8:30 P.M., it has, for parents and teachers alike, been a very long day. Wrapping things up and planning a new activity is a nice way to end it though.

So how does the workshop experience actually feel? Robbie McLoud teaches first grade at Milwaukee's La Escuela Fratney, a bilingual multicultural elementary school, and is a co-leader of our Parent Project there. Here's how she describes it:

SURVIVING (AND ENJOYING) WORKSHOP # 1
*Robbie McLoud, first-grade teacher*

After school Fratney is often filled with people: staff members trying to catch up or planning for the next day, girl scouts, basketball practice, curriculum meetings, school-based management meetings, community meetings; the list goes on and on.

For six weeks on Monday nights during November and December the library at La Escuela Fratney was filled with questions, concerns, suggestions, laughter, and warmth of a small group of parents. These parents worked together to help their children, to better understand the philosophy of Fratney, and to give much-valued input on the education of their children.

From the start the project was impressive and exciting. Children in the four-year-old kindergarten, five-year-old kindergarten, and first grade received flyers explaining and promoting the project. So many parents were interested, Mercedes and I were faced with the task of choosing fifteen parents. Parents chosen reflected the ethnic makeup of the school, were either English, Spanish speakers, or bilingual and had a child in K–4, K–5, or first grade.

I remember well the night before the first meeting. Everything was well planned; child care was arranged, treats for children and adults were bought, Mercedes and I had a good idea of what to cover, parents had been contacted to make sure they could attend, yet I found myself staring at the ceiling fretting. What if nobody came? What if something happens with the child care? What if there is no dialogue? What if . . . ? What if . . . ? What if . . . ? The next night I relearned an important lesson: Never underestimate the parents from Fratney! The parents involved in the Parent Project were dependable and vocal.

Our first meeting was spent with the parents expressing their concerns and discussing what they wanted to achieve during the six weeks of the Parent Project. That first night, like many others, we ran over the scheduled ending time. And I was afraid there would be little interaction!

Meetings included a wide variety of topics. Mary Dobbs, one of Fratney's social workers, spoke about raising self-esteem in ourselves and in children. Rita Tenorio, kindergarten teacher at La Escuela Fratney, presented the philosophy of a whole language program and we discussed how this program is implemented at Fratney. We visited the Martin Luther King Library, where the children's librarian had a program for both the children of the parents involved and us. Parents and children were then able to browse and share books in the library. Other meetings were spent discussing standardized testing, reading, writing, and how to work together to best help our children. The last of the six sessions, a potluck in the gymnasium, was spent celebrating new friendships and our success as a group of parents and teachers.

Parents were given a journal and at every meeting they spent time writing. Out of these writings came the book *Smiles are Miles Wide/Las Sonrisas Son Enormes*. Parents wrote poems about their children and the children illustrated the writings. [See Figure 1 for a sample of these pieces.] Seeing a finished product, a published book, was a wonderful way to end this chapter of the Parent Project. . . . Even as the school year draws to a close, I look forward to another year of working with children and parents.

What Robbie McLoud describes is more than a workshop schedule. Attitude? To me, it is the spirit of good will that inhabits and surrounds the time schedule. It is the total atmosphere of the experience—what might be called the *ambiance*.

*FIGURE 1*
*PARENT/CHILD COLLABORATIONS*

*Eva Diaz/Eduardo and Orlando Diaz*

. . . . . . . . . . . . . . . . . . . . . . . . . . . . . . . . . . . . . . . . . . . . . . . . . . . . . . . .

Orlando – Classroom 23

## Eduardo

**Eduardo:**
**Funny and sweet;**
**he jumps, runs, and laughs.**
**Eduardo's smiles are miles deep.**

**Eduardo:**
**Travieso, pero cariñoso;**
**brinca, corre, y ríe.**
**Las sonrisas de Eduardo son enormes.**

## Orlando

**Orlando:**
**Inquisitive, bright**
**Wonders, thinks, asks**
**Everything he says is followed**
**by an exclamation mark!**

**Orlando:**
**curioso, inteligente**
**admira, piensa, pregunta**
**¡Todo lo que dice es una exclamación!**

Eduardo – Classroom 11

## FIRST-NAME BASIS

One of the parent participants from Milwaukee's Hi-Mount Elementary School, a predominantly African-American neighborhood school, talks about the effect of using first names in the workshops:

> I always had problems in school. . . . I dropped out. I never could deal with teachers or principals. I didn't like them. But through the program, I came to appreciate the teachers, the principal, the whole faculty. I can work with them. We even call them by their first name. It breaks down the tension. I was surprised how easy it was to talk to them. It helps you appreciate teachers. To me, teachers were just someone who got paid and did their job so I didn't have to bother with teaching the kids. But it's not like that any more. (Sautter, 1991)

The bottom line is to encourage teachers and parents to be as comfortable as possible. First-name comfort level is not by any means universal, and some people find the use of first names to be a mark of disrespect. One way of furthering the intent of the workshop would be to ask participants to indicate the name they want others to call them by. "Your preferred name" could be part of the opening introductory interview. So, by "first-name basis" we are really saying that it is important to know who people are and how to acknowledge them by name.

## CO-FACILITATORS FOR
## ENERGY AND SUPPORT

In the planning stages, you may think you will be able to handle everything by yourself, but when the actual workshop is in progress, you will enjoy it much more if you have at least one other facilitator there for support and leadership. One person cannot think of everything; not only are there all the details surrounding the actual workshop to take care of (like child care, snacks), there are the small and large group discussions. Given the goals of our Project, parent/teacher leadership teams make the most sense. Many Parent Projects begin with teachers as the co-facilitators—with parent co-leaders emerging as a result of the workshops.

## OWNERSHIP

Workshop agendas need to be set with the participants. Part of the job of the workshop leaders is to provide participants with information and a structure for building the agendas. Agendas generally do not reveal themselves immediately and often become defined suddenly as an unpredicted result of another workshop activity. One very memorable example of this occurred during the second workshop of a project at Milwaukee's Sherman Elementary School. Parents and teachers had interviewed their children since the previous workshop meeting and had begun to report what they had learned. Parent after parent recounted their shock at how deeply their children had been affected by the street violence around them:

- "He said, 'If you get killed I won't have a mother, I'll just have an auntie'."
- "He's so young to be worried."
- "She's afraid she won't see the weekend."
- "Right now I can still outrun them."
- "Every half-hour you hear guns. BAM. BAM. BAM."
- "I live on Sherman. There was some kids that were fighting, and the kid ran away and got hit by a car."
- "The problem's people don't have any jobs."
- "Where's all the good people—are they all in church?"

In all of our planning for Sherman school, "Helping Children and Parents Cope with Street Violence" had never occurred to us as a workshop focus, but here it was—preeminent. For workshops to take on a life of their own, they need breathing room.

There are two aspects of ownership to honor: the individual participant and the group.

## RESPONSIBILITY IS A PARTNER OF OWNERSHIP

Ask for help with the various things that are necessary for the workshops to function. In general, teacher and parent participants want to help and they do. It is easier to volunteer for something, however, if you know exactly what is entailed and, if there is a monetary expenditure (like buying the snacks), how the money will be handled. The two most time-consuming details of the Project are arranging for child care and buying/setting up/cleaning up the refreshments. Co-leaders have plenty to do without having to tend to these details.

## THE GOLDEN RULE

The Golden Rule of the Parent Project seems to be that problem solving is more productive than blaming.

## CONSISTENCY

This applies to workshop time, place, day, and overall format. You also need to think through your stipend policy and decide whether or not participant absence from one or two workshops will affect the final stipend payment.

## CONTINUITY

The connection between workshops is usually the home activity—for instance, "catching your children doing something good" from the self-esteem workshop. Participants would then begin the next week's workshop by sharing what they "caught" their kids doing.

## CIRCLE

Sitting in a circle makes it much easier for participants to see, talk, discuss, and be themselves.

## DO

Do—don't just talk about doing.

## ALWAYS BEGIN BY BUILDING THE GROUP— OR, CONTINUITY, PART II

In a way, the start of every workshop is like starting all over again. The reasons for "reforming" the group are immediate: people need to know each other in order to work comfortably together. There are a number of strategies for reforming the group. After participants give their name and their children's names and grade level in school, you may want to ask them to do the following:

- Share one "news item" from their life.

    —or—

- Share some news about their children and school.

    —or—

- State one thing they have in common with everyone in the room, and one thing they feel is individual to them (this is a strategy described by Linda Rief in *Seeking Diversity*, 1992).

    —or—

- Name one thing that makes learning easy for them and one thing that makes it difficult (Rief, 1992).

    —or—

- State something they've done for themselves during the week (this is generally used at the start of the self-esteem workshop).

## BE PREPARED

Be prepared to start late but end on time. (Remember some people may have children to pick up from child care.)

## DON'T POSTPONE CHRISTMAS

If you are conducting a year-long program, try to pay part of the stipends before Christmas.

## EVERYONE PARTICIPATES

Everyone—including the co-facilitators, the guest presenter, and any invited observers—should participate in the workshop activities.

## TRUST IN THE GROUP DYNAMICS— SHARING AND PROBLEM SOLVING

••••••••••••••••••••••••••••••••••••••••••••••••••••••••••••••••••

Given the complicated nature of many of the issues that emerge during workshop discussions, it is unrealistic to expect that the workshop leaders will be able to supply all the answers. However, we have found that there is generally a collective wisdom and experience in the group that, if called upon with trust and openness, can begin to mediate many problems. An illustration of this happened in a third-year follow-up network meeting at Hi-Mount Elementary School. As we went around for the initial follow-up introductions, Gloria was unusually silent and distracted. She seated herself outside the group circle and seemed by the moment to become more angry and dejected. When the introductions came around to her, Gloria held up a typed letter from the Milwaukee Public School system and said that she was upset because the letter said her daughter was "mentally ill." As Gloria read part of the letter to us, she started to cry.

Teachers and some other parents in the group immediately recognized the letter as the standard form requesting parent permission to run a battery of tests to determine whether or not Gloria's daughter had a learning disability. It was the standard response of the school system to a teacher concern regarding the daughter's poor performance in school.

In spite of teacher assurances that this did not mean her daughter was "crazy" or "insane," it was the voices of other parents that soothed Gloria. Another parent explained that she had received the same letter the year before, that she had given permission for the battery of tests, that school officials had been able to diagnose her son's learning disorder and put together a program to deal with it, and that now her son was doing much better.

It is especially important that there be a flexibility built into the Parent Project schedule and structure that allows for situations like Gloria's to be voiced, discussed, and moved toward resolution.


## CLOSURE

••••••••••••••••••••••••••••••••••••••••••••••••••••••••••••••••••

Workshops don't end—they pause for a week before they resume. Before participants leave, there needs to be a consensus about what has happened and an agreement on the coming week's home/school activities.

My most vivid memory of you was your first day of school in Arizona. We had just moved 1500 miles. You had spent your first 6 years with one set of friends. Suddenly you were a stranger in a strange land. As the school bus pulled away I saw the tear ease its way down your cheek and my heart broke, knowing your pain. That same heart soars with pride as I see you handle new situations now, eight years later.

# Journals

At the beginning of our first workshop, we give all participating parents and teachers a pen and a journal. If we have some funds available, we buy the journals; in other instances, we make journals (see the sample journal cover on page 157). The optimum situation is to have parents and teachers using the same kind of journals used in the school classroom.

As we distribute the journals, we ask parents and teachers if they have ever kept a journal before and/or whether they have observed their children keeping a journal. We know that some participants will feel more comfortable with the journal than others and that in any group there will be individuals who have abandoned—or have been abandoned—by writing. We explain that since their children are using journals rather extensively in school it makes sense that parents have some idea of how journals work.

The journal is a key to the successful dynamics of the parent workshops. It is in the journal that parents keep track of workshop activities that extend from the school to the home each week. We tell parents that the journals will never be collected and exist solely for their use and that they should feel comfortable doing whatever they want to do in the journal—write, draw, make notes—any kind of notation that helps them remember what is important. It is, we stress, helpful for children to see their parents using the journal at home—not only because such use reinforces a central learning strategy, but also because it signals a life-long learning strategy. It is important that journals be introduced in a completely nonthreatening and nonjudgmental way. "Your children are using journals like these daily in their classes. Here's one for you so you can see what it's like."

After distributing the journals, we often invite participants to "freewrite" or "freedraw" for five minutes in order to get a sense of the process. Like it sounds, freewriting/drawing is supposed to be easy and without penalty. When individuals freewrite, they let the writing take on and discover its own direction. The same principle holds for freedrawing. It is important when freewriting not to be concerned with spelling, punctuation, or grammar.

Because some participants in our workshops are not comfortable with any kind of writing, free or expensive, we apply the same guidelines to freedrawing, namely, to allow the interaction of pen and paper to take on its own direction. In either case, the purpose is to facilitate a positive experience with the journal.

In our workshops, we often use freewriting/drawing as a way of focusing concerns or providing closure. We are especially careful to protect the ownership and confidentiality of such writing and drawing; it is never collected and is shared with others only when such a purpose has been clearly stated in advance.

In its "pure" form, participants freewrite/draw in their journals about whatever is on their minds. The direction the activity takes is totally up to the individual. Directed freewriting/drawing, on the other hand, is done in response to a specific topic (for instance, asking everyone to write about or draw their dreams for their children). In general, if individuals feel they can't or don't want to write or draw about the suggested topic, we invite them to journal about whatever is on their minds.

We were initially hesitant about using journals in our workshops because we did not want to make any participant feel at all uncomfortable or inadequate. At the same time, we were trusting that children in kindergarten could handle and benefit from using journals, and there seemed no logical reason to withhold such an activity from their parents.

In fact, keeping a journal quickly becomes a favorite activity of participants in our workshops. Some find using a journal to be therapeutic while others like the way it helps them organize their thoughts and feelings. Because many parents we work with lead very stressful lives, they especially appreciate the self-reflective time keeping a journal makes possible. Many say that what they like about freewriting/drawing is that it makes them feel calm. Or, as one parent said, "When I get really hot about something, I get it down in my journal and then put it in the freezer and let it cool down."

In 1990, The Joyce Foundation asked R. Craig Sautter and Sally Reid to evaluate funded parent programs in Milwaukee and Chicago. As part of the Milwaukee evaluation, Mr. Sautter interviewed a number of our parent participants. Not surprisingly, the conversation turned to the use and perceived benefits of the journal.

INTERVIEW WITH THE PARENT
PROJECT PARTICIPANTS
*(conducted by R. Craig Sautter and prepared for publication by The Joyce Foundation, 1991)*

Among the parents from Hi-Mount school who had been with the Parent Project for two years were several young women who had experienced trouble while in school and had dropped out and had children while still in their teens. Two of the women interviewed for this report live under difficult economic situations. Each also had two children in Hi-Mount and were recommended by the staff in a Chapter 1 program. Since joining the parent program, all their children have moved beyond Chapter 1. And all the children now own some of their own books, even though the parents find it expensive.

The journal was one technique that made an impression on these women.

"My third-grader got so involved in the journal," said Robinson. "She wrote page after page. She likes to make up her own little stories. She writes about school, her friends, her sister, anything that comes to her mind. She uses it every day."

"I love writing in my journal," agreed Hudson. "This class has helped me control my temper as well. Now I am much more calm. It's helped me to take a burden off of my shoulders and to feel better about myself. And I can talk quietly to my kids. I don't have to yell at them any more. Talking through my problems in this group helped. If I have a bad day, I'll just write in the journal."

"It helps a lot to talk out your problems," Herbert concurred. "Writing has helped too. If there are problems, I try to communicate with my kids or even my husband sometimes by writing notes."

Group problem-solving made a difference.

"It becomes the entire group's problem," explained Robinson. "We all tried to come up with solutions. I didn't think much of the program when I heard about it. I said, 'oh no, another stupid program to get people prying into your life again.' But then I found it was fun and helpful. Being a single parent, it is important to have someone to turn to. And because I am writing it all down in the journal, it helps me to analyze what is happening to me. I think, maybe there is a better way to handle this. Before, I didn't even think about it. I just reacted. Now I can put my energy into that book instead of striking out against my kids, or I'll just enjoy writing about a terrific day."

Children love to imitate their parents, and one of the immediate things that happens when parents start keeping their own journal is that their children want one too. In order to anticipate this need, we show parents how to make journals easily at home for their children and supply a journal cover format that can always be stapled to some sheets of blank paper (see page 157).

For parents who particularly enjoy using a journal, we describe the following options:

- *The Personal Journal.* This is kept separately by parent and child. It is a place for personal thoughts, creations, and reflections. Some parents set aside five or ten minutes in the evening at home for "journal time" with their children. We emphasize that it is important to work out privacy rules for these journals in advance, and it is our belief that parent and child have the right to keep personal journal entries private.

- *Dialogue Journal.* This is a written conversation between parent and child. Dialogue journals can be ongoing or caused by a specific event, such as a field trip or a traumatic or happy incident. Dialogue journals are also useful for family problem solving.

Many parents are already keeping a kind of dialogue journal with their children without realizing it. "Oh, you mean that little pad of paper next to the phone?"

An extremely useful extension of the dialogue journal—especially given the philosophy of the Parent Project—is to arrange for written conversations between parent, child, and teacher. These three-way dialogues seem to work best when they have a specific focus, such as responses to reading books, classroom projects, and evaluations and grades.

- *Your Children—Life and Times.* In this journal the parent becomes a historian of significant events—large and small—in their child's life. In order to get started, we suggest that parents write this journal as if they are writing a letter directly to their child. Some parents give these "histories" as presents at important events in their children's lives—graduation, marriage, the birth of a child. Some parents write weekly, some monthly, some every few months. A schedule isn't the point, but rather the feeling that something needs to be shared and remembered.

Camille Thalman/Michael Thalman

I remember...

The night you were born,
in a hurry, no time to wait...

Baby Magic lotion and the
feel of your soft, lotion-scented
skin at my breast...

The first time you let go of
my hand, to toddle wobbly
on your own...

Innocent, smiling eyes as
you sat clean, toweled and
robed, back in your red
bath tub of water...

The effort and determination
etched on your brow as you
tried over and over to climb
the "mountainous" hill in front
of our home...

Your sweet abandon once
you accomplished this and
countless other tasks along
the way...

My joy at discovering, though
you hated my attempts to
sing you to sleep, we shared
a love of books and reading...

The millions of peanut butter
and jelly (grape, of course!) sandwiches
you have consumed...

Your first day of school,
shy and small, scared and
curious all at once...

My pride as I caught a
glimpse of you riding a bicycle
for the first time, on your own...

The warm, special
feeling I get when
you wrap your
arms around me
and say, "I love
you, Mom

I ♥ U MOM

MICHAEL

by Camille
Thalman

*Migdalia Rivera/Ingrid Rivera*

Ingrid

Cariñosa y alegre.
Me gusta pintar, y me gusta
mucho escribir en mi pizarra,
y me gusta jugar con mis muñecas.
Mi palabra favorita es Rabbit.

Ingrid Chakira.

Ingrid
  Affectionate and cheerful
I like to paint and I very much
like to write on my blackboard,
and I like to play with my dolls.
My favorite word is Rabbit.
  Ingrid Chakira

# Circle
## Of
### Belief

We initiated the Parent Project with a certain sense of belief: belief that parents would respond as positively to authentic learning strategies as their children; belief that a workshop structure would build a sense of self and community; belief that, although we lacked answers to many problems, we could call upon the resources of workshop participants to move toward these answers.

Sometimes things happen the way they are supposed to happen; other times they don't. Sometimes things all come together in the most unexpected ways, like the fire-safety workshop at Hi-Mount Elementary School.

Milwaukee is a city of multiple-story frame houses. Every winter a number of these homes become the scenes of fiery death—the casualties often very young children. It was after a series of such fires in the Hi-Mount area that workshop participants decided to focus one meeting on fire safety.

We arranged for a local fire fighter to come in and give a guest presentation, part of which consisted of a horrific videotape. Through the ensuing small and large group discussions, the home activity for the coming week began to define itself. The videotape emphasized how important it was to have an escape route clearly mapped and understood by everyone in the family in the event of a fire, and during the coming week each of us was to try to meet with everyone in our home space, map an escape route in our journals, practice the route, and note responses in our journals. We had anticipated that the videotape would also renew interest in smoke detectors and fire extinguishers, and we purchased one detector and extinguisher for each participant who needed them—which turned out to be everyone. Participants were also asked to install the detectors and extinguishers in addition to planning an escape route with their families.

A few weeks later, one of the parents told the workshop that a fire broke out in her kitchen, and that, using the new extinguisher, she had put it out. One of the teachers remarked that the woman's son had been writing about the incident in school, and she showed us a picture the child had drawn of orange flames bursting out the windows and chimney of the house and two figures yelling "help" through the open windows. Above the picture was written:

## HERO
*BY ANTEREL*

My mom is a hero .she saved someones life the wanmons who life she save was glade . a hero is a person who save someone life in rise there life for another person life .

the end

For one clear moment, it all seemed to come together—school and home, parent, child, teacher, and community.

# Beyond Workshop 1: A Three-Year Plan

A fully developed Parent Project involves three initiatives:

1. *Initial Workshop Series (Six 2- to 2.5-Hour Sessions)*

   This is the six-week workshop for parents who have not previously participated. This often involves parents with children in K–1.

2. *Follow-up Network*

   Monthly workshops for parents and teachers who have participated in the Initial Workshop Series. If numbers of participants become too great for group work, follow-up groups can be divided by grade level or special interest.

3. *Leadership Institute*

   There needs to be a mechanism to identify, support, and train parent leaders to co-facilitate Initial Workshop Series and follow-up sessions.

How these three aspects of the Parent Project interact is distinct to the individual school, agency, or constituency. A very general overview would be:

YEAR ONE

- As many Initial Workshop Series as possible.
- Monthly Follow-Up Network commencing after completion of first six-week workshop series.

TRANSITION BETWEEN YEAR ONE AND YEAR TWO

- Leadership Institute

YEAR TWO

- As many Initial Workshop Series as possible.
- Monthly Follow-Up Network.

TRANSITION BETWEEN YEAR TWO AND YEAR THREE

- Leadership Institute

- As many Initial Workshop Series as possible.
- Monthly Follow-Up Network
- Evaluation of effectiveness of Parent Project with resetting of short- and long-range goals.

## FOLLOW-UP

The monthly follow-up workshops give longevity to the Parent Project. They are the place for problem solving, support, agenda setting, and renewed friendship. Here's a description of the process from my journal as the follow-up network convened at the beginning of our third year at Hi-Mount Elementary School:

*Sept. 18.* We began by asking everyone to relate their summer "news." Three more parents returned to school to get their high school equivalency, and Shandra gave birth to her third child. Alice announced her "news" by saying that she has become "calm." She also enrolled in courses at MATC and decided to pursue her dream of becoming a paralegal. Everyone applauded. We've been encouraging Alice in this direction. Alice said that keeping a journal is what helped her achieve her new sense of "calm."

We asked teachers and parents what kind of workshops and activities they would like to be involved in during the year. "Discipline," "math," "how to use the computers," "self-esteem," "the new report cards," "another published book." Year 3 had begun.

The sense of community formed during the initial six-week workshop series is clearly one of the prime motivations for parents and teachers to become involved in the monthly follow-up workshops. As with Alice from my journal entry, a lot of it has to do with simply knowing that there is this group of people there on Tuesday night who know you have been struggling with the hope of becoming a paralegal and who are going to be really excited when you finally announce your news.

We have found that it is easier for everyone to remember the follow-up workshop days and time if we schedule them in a consistent way, for instance, the second Tuesday of each month at 6:30 P.M. The basic dynamic of the follow-up workshops is similar to the initial workshop series:

- Reforming the group.
- Guest presentation on topic of group interest.
- Hands-on work involving session focus.
- Small and large group discussion of relevant home activities.
- Agreement on activities for parents and children to try before the next follow-up meeting.

Of course, the same support structure for all workshops also applies to the follow-up sessions: namely, child care, refreshments at break, transportation, materials, and supplies. Stipends seem to be less of an incentive at the follow-up stage of the Parent Project.

After the initial year of the Parent Project, follow-up sessions can be rather large, and (given resources) you may need to offer more than one follow-up meeting time per month—say, the second Tuesday evening and the first Saturday morning of each month. Like all workshops, follow-up sessions tend to take on their own distinct identity per school site. Hi-Mount Elementary School, for example, is a computer-specialty school, which means that children use computers on a daily basis in all classrooms, including kindergarten. There was a clear desire by Hi-Mount parents to make "How to Use the Computer" the focus of a series of follow-up sessions. At Kagel Elementary School on Milwaukee's south side, on the other hand, there was a follow-up interest in health issues such as lead poisoning.

In other words, follow-up sessions breathe; they expand and contract. Participants—teachers and parents—may disappear from the follow-up part of the Parent Project for months (or even years) only to return when their circumstances make it possible.

The ongoing follow-up structure gives everyone time to fully develop and explore ideas, and it is not unusual to return again and again to issues like self-esteem, reading, writing, and academic persistence. Because we feel the published collections of teacher/parent/child collaborative work is so important, we also try to publish a book at least once a year in each follow-up network.

Since participation in follow-up workshops varies more than in the initial six-week workshop series, reforming the group at the start of each follow-up meeting is especially important. We usually start off by going around and asking for two news items: 1) personal news about the parent or teacher participant ("I have no personal news, I'm a teacher." "I've got no personal news either. I'm a parent."), and 2) some news about how their children are doing in school. Sharing personal news and school news can take thirty minutes to an hour, and it is time well spent—often leading to future workshop topics.

An interesting thing that often happens in the follow-up sessions is a shift in focus from children to parents. Parents become interested in their own education, their own choices. I remember one parent at Sherman Elementary School who asked, during the introductory part of a follow-up session, whether people thought she was too old to go back to school. "How old are you?" a number of us asked. "Twenty-nine," came the answer. To believe in follow-up is to believe in the future.

## LEADERSHIP INSTITUTE

A flourishing follow-up network for each Parent Project site is also essential to identifying and supporting parents and teachers who want to take on leadership responsibilities for the Project. Leadership is an often illusive quality that depends a great deal on opportunity, support, and timing. Regardless of the size of the Parent Project, there are numerous opportunities for leadership, and we encourage participants to take on whatever kinds of responsibilities they are comfortable with. One parent at Hi-Mount Elementary School, for example, decided to keep a dialogue journal with her third-grade son as a kind of "pilot dialogue journal" for other participants; a parent at Kagel Elementary School began to work with her son's teacher in the classroom; a parent at Sherman Elementary School became president of the PTO.

We invite parent and teacher participants from the six-week workshop series and the follow-up network to take part in the Leadership Institute. Our goals in the Leadership Institute are to support parents and teachers in whatever ways they want to make a positive difference and to identify co-facilitators for the ongoing workshops—entry level and follow-up. Unlike the two-hour format we use for the six-week and follow-up workshops, we try to hold the Leadership Institute for two full days (9-3). To get two full days either involves an act of God or summer vacation, and we've found summer to be a flexible time for our institute.

The primary rhythm of the Leadership Institute involves participants' reflection, goal setting, and plan of action for themselves, their children, the school site, and the Parent Project. Because of their other Parent Project workshop experiences, many participants of the

Leadership Institute know each other and enjoy working together. Our most successful institutes give future co-facilitators opportunities to design and conduct a workshop based on a perceived need of their respective school site. Every teacher and job applicant knows that you never get another chance to make a first impression, and so for participants who intend to co-facilitate Parent Project workshops, we also discuss and role-play the Introductory Community-Building Workshop (see page 58).

We have found that stipends play a significant role in leadership development. We are asking parents and teachers to commit a lot of energy and time over a period of years with our Project, and it is unrealistic (and unfair) to expect individuals to continue to make this a part of their life without monetary acknowledgment.

In bilingual school sites, we are especially interested in supporting bilingual facilitator teams. In large Parent Project sites, in which there may be six or seven co-facilitator teams, we usually schedule a time for all the co-facilitators to meet (and probably have lunch or dinner). We do everything we can to honor and reward school co-facilitator leadership teams; they *are* our sense of possibility.

Buitful

mona
Rae
Olmstead

6 year old

Mona

helpful--shares
Reads, runs, cleans-up
She likes to be of help and she play
with her sister

doll

# Workshops Anyone?

As time goes on, the workshop focus becomes more specific. In terms of the initial six-week workshop series, we have found definite patterns of interest—particularly issues involving writing, reading, and self-esteem. There is, as well, what I will term a *special interest* workshop, the focus of which is site-specific. Special interest workshops respond to the priority need of the specific parent/teacher workshop group (for instance, fire safety, how to use the computer, lead poisoning, standardized testing, the new report card, violence in and out of the school, discipline issues). Since each six-week workshop series also contains an introductory community-building workshop and a final closure/celebration, the basic six-week workshop topic focus often looks like this:

- WEEK ONE:      Introductory Community-Building Workshop
- WEEK TWO:      Reading Workshop
- WEEK THREE:  Writing Workshop
- WEEK FOUR:    Self-Esteem Workshop
- WEEK FIVE:      Special-Interest Workshop
- WEEK SIX:        Closure/Celebration Workshop

Practically speaking, focus and strategy do not begin and end with each particular workshop session, but rather recur, deepen, and evolve throughout the series. Thus, we try to incorporate journal writing and shared reading of children's books in all workshops. Reading and writing activities also enhance self-esteem, which in turn impacts almost every issue—including assessment.

What follows are some of the workshops we've facilitated in each category.

## INTRODUCTORY COMMUNITY-BUILDING WORKSHOP

The first meeting of the Parent Project needs to accomplish a number of things, foremost among them, building a sense of shared purpose and ownership of the ongoing workshop process. One of the best ways of accomplishing this is to have participants interview each other and then introduce the person they interview to the entire group. The first workshop is also the place to distribute journals (in which participants can keep notes for the interview-introductions) and elicit the agenda concerns of the group. The first workshop sets the tone for all the workshops to follow, so don't forget to arrange the seating in a circle so everyone can see each other.

I've tried to outline the first workshop in terms of how the two hours of time can be apportioned for the activities.

## WELCOME (10 minutes)

Briefly identify co-facilitators and go over dates and times of workshop sessions.

Distribute journals and explain that they should be used in whatever way that's comfortable—for notes, drawing, details, whatever. Ask parents if they have observed their children keeping journals.

The focus of this workshop is for parents and teachers to become more familiar with each other and to do some agenda building.

## INTERVIEW INTRODUCTIONS (60 minutes)

Parent and teacher participants work in pairs interviewing each other. After the interviews are completed, participants will introduce the person they interviewed to the whole group.

Before the interviewing begins, generate possible questions from the whole group: name, hobbies, children's ages and names, occupations and pursuits; one thing the individual has in common with everyone else in the group, and one thing that is unique to them; where they live, how they feel about being in the workshop, and so on.

Each person should spend five minutes interviewing their partner—ten minutes total. Co-facilitators should also take part in the interview process. People can use their journals to help them remember the specifics of their interviews.

After the ten minutes are up, reform the whole group, and go around the circle having each person introduce the individual they interviewed.

## BREAK (10 minutes)

You will probably want to break before all of the interview introductions are completed.

## WORKSHOP PROCESS *(10 minutes)*

• • • • • • • • • • • • • • • • • • • • • • • • • • • • • • • • • • • • • • • • • • • • • • • • • • • • • •

After the introductions are completed, talk a little about the workshop process and ask participants what concerns they would like addressed in the coming workshops. Make a list and use this information in future scheduling.

## EXPLANATION OF JOURNALS *(20 minutes)*

• • • • • • • • • • • • • • • • • • • • • • • • • • • • • • • • • • • • • • • • • • • • • • • • • • • • • •

Now that everyone has their own journal it's time to talk. Ask one or more teachers to briefly explain (through actual student examples from their classrooms) how journals work at varying grade and development levels. Show parents how to make a journal for their children at home.

## HOME APPLICATIONS *(10 minutes)*

• • • • • • • • • • • • • • • • • • • • • • • • • • • • • • • • • • • • • • • • • • • • • • • • • • • • • •

Discuss home applications. Ask participants to interview one or more of their children during the week and to make notations of the interviews in their journals.

Generate some possible questions for parent/child interviews.

Take this time to check on whether anyone has transportation problems. Are there possibilities for car pooling?

*INTERVIEW/INNER VIEW* • The interview is a structured conversation between parent and child memorialized through the journal. Parents enjoy interviewing their children because they often learn things about their children that they didn't know before. Children like the interviews because the format bestows a sense of importance upon them. For many parents and children, caught up in the rush of every day activities, the interview process reaffirms the benefits of taking time to ask questions and listen to answers.

*NOTES FROM AN INTERVIEW BETWEEN A MOTHER AND SON*

*Q:* What do you like the best about your school?

*A:* Some of the good classes I have and after-school sports.

*Q:* What do you dislike about your school?

*A:* Too much violence around the school.

Q: What do you like doing with our family the most?

A: I like going over to my cousins and other families' homes (relatives' homes).

Q: What do you want to do when you grow up?

A: Next question. You know I'm confused about that one, Mom.

Q: Favorite toy?

A: Remote control cars—planes, trains, helicopters, and stuff like that.

Q: Favorite TV show?

A: The Disney Afternoon.

Q: Favorite foods?

A: French toast, cheese burgers, cookies, french fries, fish fillets.

Q: Favorite people and best friends?

A: Kiya, Johnny Smith, Danny, Fresh Prince, Jazzy Jeff.

Q: Things you like best in life are?

A: Playing the piano, putting trains together, playing with cars and friends, making things.

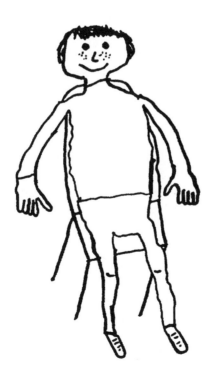

Q: What kinds of things do you worry about?

A: Getting jumped after school, getting lost, friends and family dying.

Q: Favorite places you like to go?

A: McDonalds, Chuck E Cheese, Johnson's Park, bowling, movies, field trips, parks, out of town.

Q: Who do you admire most?

A: My great-grandmother who died. I always think about her, and sometimes she's even in my dreams. My father and mother—alive.

Q: How do you feel about this interview?

A: I feel I could go on and on. It is fun!

Q: What do you think the Parent class is doing for me?

A: I think it is telling you about what I like.

## READING WORKSHOPS

We try to read aloud a children's book every time we meet. Part of the reason for this is that children's books are such an enjoyable way to focus ideas and build a sense of community; part of the reason is that we also want to expand parents' sense of the range of children's books available and the different ways of enjoying these books with their children. As with writing, the comfort level of participants is paramount. In multilingual groups, we make every effort to present books in different languages and to offer summary translations of these books when they are read aloud. In groups in which there are parents who do not read, we explore the possibilities of wordless picture books and telling stories through a book's illustrations.

Reading workshops rekindle interest in children's books and in reading itself for many parent participants. The discussion about reading between parents Angela Hudson and Bonnie Robinson from the Sautter/Reid interview underscores the way reading together enhances the relationship between parent and child:

"It [Parent Project] has taught me a lot," said Angela Hudson. "I learned how to sit down and read with my children, to take fifteen minutes with one child, while the other two do something else. I do it every night, no matter what. If I forget, they will remind me. They love it. We also take trips to the library, even in the winter."

"I didn't read to my kids and the only time they saw me read was when I picked up the Sunday or Wednesday paper," said Bonnie

Robinson. "But once I got involved in the program, they made me see that it was important so I started reading to my kids. Now my six-year-old gets a book and says, 'Mama, read to me, read to me.' They enjoyed it so much that I said, 'OK, OK.' I do it, because even I enjoy it now. Before, I didn't care for it. Now my kids say, 'Oh, Mama likes to read, so maybe we should do it, maybe it is fun.' Before my eight-year-old didn't enjoy it either and wasn't very good at it. Now she is much better and wants to read."

*Blanca Tran/Uy H Tran*

UY H TRAN

Inquieto y cariñoso
Corre, brinca, y sonrie,
y las sonrisas de Uy
Son enormes y amorosas
Llenas de calor.

My techer is reaDing a Book to Me in s School.

UY H TRAN

Restless and loving
He runs, jumps, and smiles
Uy's smiles
are huge and affectionate
Filled with warmth.

## READING WORKSHOP 1: INTRODUCING A FAVORITE CHILDREN'S BOOK

• • • • • • • • • • • • • • • • • • • • • • • • • • • • • • • • • • • • • • • • • • • • • • • • • • •

The range of possible reading workshops is as large as the number of good children's books out there. One of the more interesting ways of entering into a reading workshop is to have participants bring a favorite children's book to one of the sessions. The book can be from their own childhood, or a favorite of one of their children, or perhaps one the teacher has read aloud in class. Or, it might even be a new favorite found during the week in the library (especially after we've taken the library "field trip" discussed in "Reading Workshop 4").

Start, then, reforming the group by asking each person to introduce themselves by introducing the book they have brought with them. Individuals who forget to bring a children's book can talk instead about a favorite they remember, or a family story, or how their kids seem to feel about reading. The idea is to get everyone talking and thinking about books, and when you are finished going around the group, there will be a wealth of information about reading. Not only will there be a range of children's books spanning three to four generations, but also there will be a renewed sense of the significance of reading and being read to. As participants talk about their favorite children's book, they will inevitably talk about reading—how they read and how they were read to. Ways of sharing books at home gradually emerge as individuals hold up the book they have brought and start to talk about it: memories of sitting on a parent's lap while reading, of taking turns with different passages, of inventing stories based on the book's illustrations. If the school site has a Reading Specialist on the staff, he or she can serve as a guest presenter.

Another way of entering into a reading workshop entails prolonged involvement with and enjoyment of a specific children's book. It's even more interesting when the main characters of the book are parents, teachers, and children. Two such books, which lend themselves to very different kinds of workshops, are *The Wednesday Surprise*, and *Today Was a Terrible Day*. (All children's books discussed here are included in the bibliography of children's books that begins on page 164.)

## READING WORKSHOP 2: CAPTURING THE SURPRISE IN THE WEDNESDAY SURPRISE

• • • • • • • • • • • • • • • • • • • • • • • • • • • • • • • • • • • • • • • • • • • • • • • • • • •

I hold up *The Wednesday Surprise* by Eve Bunting and ask parents and teachers what they think the book is about.* The cover

---

*The inspiration for this workshop came from Smokey Daniels.

illustration by Donald Carrick is a cozy one in which a bespectacled elderly woman holds a book and a young girl sits next to her on an old-fashioned couch. Both the woman and the girl are looking carefully at the book open in front of them. Their laps are covered by a brightly colored quilt, and the girl holds a cat in her free hand.

"What do you think this *Wednesday Surprise* could be about?" I ask.

- "A party."
- "It's in the book she's holding."
- "The cat. The cat's named Wednesday."
- "It's really Tuesday."
- "The grandchild gets read to on Wednesdays."
- "They're reading about a surprise that's going to happen on a Wednesday."
- "Grandma's in a Parent Project."

I ask about the relationship between the young girl and the older woman. "Grandmother reading to granddaughter on Wednesdays" is the gathering consensus.

I read the book aloud. The story is told through the point of view of the young girl, Anna. On Wednesday nights Anna and her grandmother read books in preparation for Dad's birthday surprise. Most first-time readers assume the surprise to be that the grandmother has taught Anna to read. Not until the evening of Dad's birthday do we learn that it is Grandma who has learned to read. In fact, Grandma reads up a storm for Dad's birthday. *The Wednesday Surprise* ends triumphantly:

"Maybe I will read everything in the world now that I've started," Grandma says in a stuck up way. "I've got time." She winks at me.

"So, Anna? What do you think? Was it a good surprise?"

"I run to her and she puts her cheek against mine. "The best ever," I say.

As we finish the book I ask all participants to write and/or draw a response to the story in their journals. I tell them that we are going to divide into pairs and respond to each other's journal entry. Once everyone has a partner, I ask them to exchange journals and respond to what the first person has written about the book. The pair then exchange their journals one more time and the first person responds to the second person's comments.

When everyone has finished their dialogues, I ask how people felt about it. The general response is that exchanging journals is fun and interesting. I ask if any pair wants to share what theirs was about, and the response ranges from the very personal ("my grandmother died last week") to the very philosophical ("the story gives dignity to people other people term 'illiterate'").

After break, I return to *The Wednesday Surprise* in order to show parents how different reading strategies work with the book. I begin with the cover illustration and the general consensus that a grandmother and granddaughter were depicted. I ask if there is anything in the illustration that made readers conclude that it was the grandmother who was doing the teaching.

We *discuss* strategies such as how well the book lends itself to *pausing* in the reading and *predicting*. I reread a few separate episodes and ask how people felt at those particular points in the story. And what did they think was going to happen? I explain how one of the main things that motivates reading involves *guessing* about what's going to happen next and then discovering what does happen.

*Prediction* is a crucial reading strategy for parents to enjoy with their children. If both parent and child are reading the book for the first time, then pausing for prediction and discussion is spontaneous fun. We also talk about how rereading *The Wednesday Surprise* deepens and complicates the original experience. One person points out the opening anxiety of Anna being home alone without adult supervision before Grandma's arrival; someone mentions the fact that both parents work and that the working class setting is appealing; someone points out that the birthday gifts that are exchanged don't cost money. There are many comments about the reversal of expectation in the book, how it's never too late to learn, how adults can learn from kids—parents from their children, teachers from their students.

We list some of the things that have happened through our reading and examination of *The Wednesday Surprise*:

- journaling
- predicting
- retelling
- questioning
- talking
- rereading
- pausing and discussing
- reflecting

There is no advantage in belaboring these reading strategies. Nothing is gained when the joy of reading is replaced by the self-conscious "reading lesson." The main thing is that we want parents to understand some of the options for sharing books with their children.

We call the activity for the week "The Everyday Surprise." We ask teachers to make some journal notations of things they learn from students during the coming week. And parents are asked to note what they learn from their children. We will share some of these journal entries at the start of our next workshop. Here is an entry from teacher Jeanette MacMurdo's journal:

KIDWATCHING JOURNAL, APRIL 26, 1989
*Jeanette MacMurdo*

Today I watched Jeff, who frequently suffers from depression. Our task today was to find words and phrases the author used to set the mood and tone of the story. The class was very much into the activity, including Jeff. By the time I passed behind him he also had several phrases. When I commented on his excellent choices, he smiled. I asked him how one of his particular phrases made him feel and he responded quickly. He continued his search and was very selective. During their small group sharing time he was participating and added a selected few of his peers' choices. He willingly shared his favorite example during whole class sharing.

I guess I must conclude that once I can get Jeff started on an activity he will work as long as he is challenged. Since this was an activity with much freedom for choosing answers, he felt he could express his individuality. I need to find activities that are a challenge for him and allow him to do more interpretative reactions to what he reads.

## READING WORKSHOP 3: RECLAIMING THE TERRIBLE DAY—A READING-TO-WRITE/ WRITING-TO-READ WORKSHOP

● ● ● ● ● ● ● ● ● ● ● ● ● ● ● ● ● ● ● ● ● ● ● ● ● ● ● ● ● ● ● ● ● ● ● ● ● ● ● ● ● ● ● ● ● ● ● ● ● ● ● ● ● ● ● ● ● ● ● ● ● ●

In *Today Was a Terrible Day*, by Patricia Reilly Giff and illustrated by Susanna Natti, second-grader Ronald Morgan has one of those days at school in which everything goes wrong. Ronald forges his mother's signature on a note, he loses his recess baseball game, he fails the forced public basal recitation, and he knocks the teacher's plant on the floor in his haste to remember his job as class "plant monitor."

As a workshop focus, *Today Was a Terrible Day* provides a good opportunity for everyone to discuss some of their children's problems in school and to discuss these problems in an open and understanding atmosphere. Ronald's plight also reminds some of us of our own experiences in school. At the conclusion of the story, Ronald's teacher writes him a note to boost his spirits.

After discussing the note and Ronald's difficulties with reading (a later book in the series reveals that he's dyslexic), I invite participants to write a note to one or more of their children. The purpose of the note is to achieve the same kind of "ego boost" effect that Ronald experiences in the book. I distribute stamped envelopes so that workshop members can address and actually mail their letters.

When we meet the next week, parents and teachers share the results of the letters. For many of the children, this marks the first official "mail" from their parents. One of the parents passes around a letter she received back from her children (shown in Figure 2).

FIGURE 2
CHILDREN'S LETTER RESPONSE

....................................................................

"Mom you are the best. I like what you do for me. And when you gave Domique and me a note. I feel happy so was Domique. And mom me and Domique still love you."

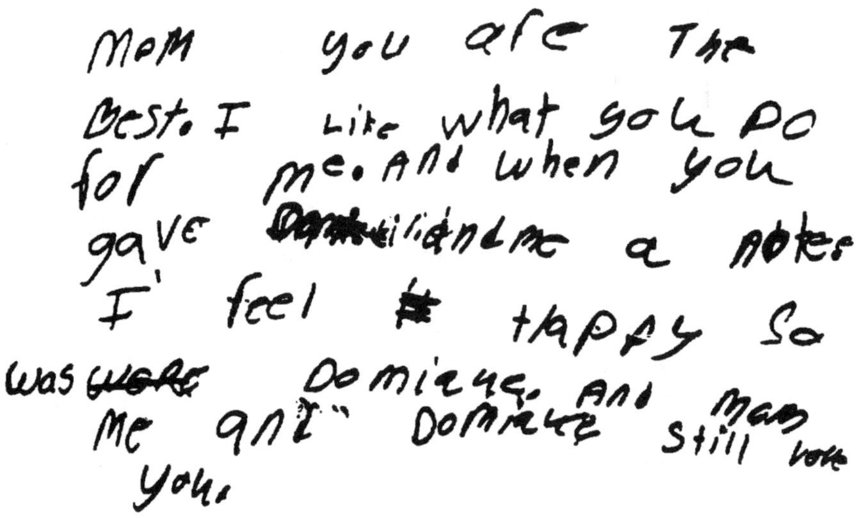

## READING WORKSHOP 4: READING-TO-GO— CHECKING OUT THE LIBRARY

The library "field trip" generally takes an entire two-hour workshop session. If you contact the local public library sufficiently in advance, they can probably arrange for a presentation by a librarian. In addition to such a presentation, it is important for there to be time for parents to have their questions answered and for a general exploration of the facilities. This is a good session to have children accompany their parents.

The biggest problem in arranging the library field trip is transportation. Sometimes we meet at the library; other times we meet at the school site and car pool (or, if the library is close, walk) from there.

We are going to ask parents to return to the library the week after the field trip and check out some books with their children, so be sure to tell parents who do not have a library card to bring proof of residency—like a telephone bill addressed to them. You may encounter some parents who already have library cards but have stopped using them because of outstanding fines. Sometimes we have been successful in getting the library to grant an amnesty.

We begin the following week's workshop by asking participants to show us one of the books they checked out with their children and tell us a little about it. One of the most memorable experiences in our five years of workshops at Hi-Mount Elementary School occurred during this session when it came Belinda Hughes' turn to speak.

A slender, intense mother of two children, one in kindergarten and one in second grade, Belinda had been reserved and skeptical in previous workshops. This night was different, however, and when it was her turn, Belinda told us that the past week marked the first time she had read a book to her children. Belinda said that she had been brought up to believe that it was the duty of parents *not* to interfere with school—that school and home were meant to be separate. Although she had wanted to share books with her children before, Belinda also wanted to be a good parent. "It's a joy," she said, reaching for a children's book to share with all of us.

## WRITING WORKSHOPS

We initially wanted to include a writing workshop as a means of informing parents about how writing was being taught and supported in school. Because their children were publishing their own books in the classroom, we also wanted to give parents a sense of how exciting that experience could be. Parents enjoy both structured and unstructured writing activities and seem especially motivated when the subject is their children.

Some parents are going to be uncomfortable with writing and may prefer to work with another parent or teacher, or record their message for transcription. By whatever means, it is the message that's important, not its formal accoutrements. Having children illustrate their parents' writing with self-portraits has proven to be a moving and joyous experience. What follow are four workshops that can (but do not necessarily need to) lead to publication. (Also see the "Becoming Me" writing activity in the "Self-Esteem Workshop 1" on "Change.")

## I REMEMBER: A STORYTELLING WORKSHOP

Tonight's focus is writing and Elise, the school's third-grade teacher, shares different stages of writing from her classroom and passes around books her students have published. We talk about stories, and how some of the best ones are those that are true. A parent and a teacher read Angela Johnson's *Tell Me a Story, Mama* aloud. We talk about family stories—the kind that are repeated through the years.

Our workshop involves everyone in recording their favorite memory of one or more of their children. Some parents work in groups and some alone. Four parents compose on the computer and two relate their memories into a tape recorder for later transcription. Parents and teachers work together, and there is no embarrassment about different levels of writing skills.

We share the writings in small groups, and two parents read their memories to us all. Before our next meeting, parents are to share their memories with their children and encourage their children to draw illustrations. The illustrated memories will ultimately be published as our Parent Project book. (See the samples shown in Figures 3 through 6.) At our final workshop meeting, copies of the book will be distributed to parents and children as a way of celebrating collaboration, authorship, writing, and storytelling.

When you distribute the completed publications, allow time for parents to look through and enjoy them. It's fun to go around the group and ask for observations and comments. Some parents may want to autograph their copies for one another. The children's copies of the publication could be wrapped and presented to them as a gift. Discuss other kinds of illustrated books parents can make with their children. What other kinds of "true" family stories do parents often tell their children? Couldn't these stories also become illustrated books?

*FIGURE 3*
*LISA: AN ILLUSTRATED MEMORY*

*Karen Matchulat/Lisa Matchulat*

. . . . . . . . . . . . . . . . . . . . . . . . . . . . . . . . . . . . . . . . . . . . . . . . . . . . . . . . . .

*LISA*
*By Karen Matchulat*

*Each year passes more quickly, the memories start to blur in all the activity. But when I see you sleeping and kiss you goodnight I remember ...*

*The night before I took you home from the hospital, you held my finger so tight while you nursed. Your skin was so soft and even though you were small I never felt a greater love. I often think about that image when I'm relaxing.*

*As a toddler, you used to put all your clothes in a line on your bedroom floor. You'd wear whichever pants and shirt were next in line. In a strange way, I see how this was an insight into your ability to organize yourself now.*

*Your first year of school stands out in my memories, not for your many successes but for your difficulty in adjusting to day care. My heart broke when you were sad, but in time you adjusted.*

*The first time you demonstrated that you could read. I was sure you had memorized the book, until I realized you were saying all the words correctly. I was shocked and elated. You've come so far in your reading abilities in only a few short years.*

*I can't imagine what memories the next years will produce.*

FIGURE 4
MEMORIES OF CHILDREN

*Jeanie Ahrens (teacher)*

. . . . . . . . . . . . . . . . . . . . . . . . . . . . . . . . . . . . . . . . . . . . . . . . . . . . . . . . . . . . . . . . . . . . . . . . . . . . . . . . . . . . . . . . . . . . .

Memories of Children

The tongue-in-cheek saying goes, "Old teachers never die . . . they just lose their class." What a fallacy. Hundreds of children have passed through my classrooms and many of them have remained as special memories.

I think of the children in my very first class, graduating mid-year on a Friday and teaching that Monday. I was getting married at Easter and the children decided to give me a shower. Jeanne collected money right under my nose, convinced that I would never guess her secret purpose. She always told the other children she had been "named after me" because I once baby-sat for her. She was about six months old and never woke up in her crib. My students were invited to the wedding and one of the pictures shows another girl, Colleen, leaning out in the church aisle, anxious to see her teacher.

Then there was Caroline, one of my most special memories. Caroline did things in different ways than other children and never seemed to care what others thought of her. Incredibly gifted, she fit perfectly the expression "marching to a different drummer." Her eight-year-old wisdom made me think in new ways about many of the "truths" I'd been taught to believe about teaching and learning. A year later, I was given a special birthday present from Caroline. The elementary school had closed that June, each of us ending up at different schools. On my birthday, her school band played a concert at my new school and she took the time to seek me out.

Jack fits in a different memory location. He and his younger brother were only at the school for two months. Looking like little waifs, they never had time to adjust and never did quite fit in with the other children. One day, Jack's father took him out of school without time to let him gather the few school possessions he'd had time to accumulate. He was taking them to Mexico where he hoped to find a miracle cure for his cancer. That was the last I heard of Jack but I've often wondered how his life turned out.

Another bittersweet memory with a happier ending is Jason. He came to me without any indication of learning problems but it was soon evident that Jason would not find success without some special intervention. Testing revealed that Jason's intelligence level was far below what is considered normal and he was placed in a special education class. The most difficult thing I ever had to do as a teacher was to explain to the other children in my class, with tears in my eyes, why Jason wouldn't be in our room anymore, although they would see him in the building. Being children, and far more perceptive than we often think, they knew Jason had been different as far as his learning and also knew they could still be friends at recess and outside school. Jason excelled in the special program and achieved beyond our dreams.

Lisa will live forever, not only in my memory, but also in my heart. She was indeed the "one in a million." By this time I was teaching in the gifted/talented program, thanks to Caroline's inspiration. The other girls in her g/t class were more academically gifted, but Lisa had many gifts. She was wondrously creative—words and images just flowed when she wrote. She had won many awards for her figure skating. One of my special treats recently was seeing her picture on the front page of the Milwaukee Journal with an article touting her abilities at Olympic trials. Lisa's true gift, however, was her ever-sunny outlook on life. She saw good in everyone and delighted in all aspects of life. To use a trite saying, she truly was "a breath of fresh air."

Those not in teaching will never know how much our lives become entwined with these children we call "ours," even though it is only for a short while. We cry for them and cheer for them and laugh with them just as their parents do. When asked if I have any children, I guess I should answer, "Yes, hundreds, of all ages!"

Jeanie Ahrens

*FIGURE 5*
*A FATHER–DAUGHTER STORY*

*Jefferie E. Scott/Amanda Warr*

A Father - Daughter Story

Isn't she lovely
Isn't she wonderful
yes she's my little girl Amanda
She's so helpful & always willing to be your
friend.
I remember when we first met at the age
of four, I was know as Scott
She was quiet but still had that or a
of confidence.
As our relationship grew, so did our love
& trust for each other
  I would look at cartoons in the mornings
with her & she would look at Jeopardy with
me in the after noons
We now have a very loving & honest relationship
I'm know longer called Scott, but DADDY
especially when she wants something (smile)
Isn't that how daughters get what they
want from their father.

Jefferie E. Scott
Amanda's Dad.

FIGURE 6
RECUERDOS DE JONATHAN

*Maria Pedraza/Jonathan Pedraza*

Recuerdos de Jonathan

Recordamos un niño gordito
y muy activo
Siempre buscando travesuras que hacer

Recordamos como lloras cuando vas
al dentista.
Pero al llegar a la oficina que
valiente eres.

Recordamos un bebito que no hablaba
ahora con mucho orgullo hablas
español y ingles
Que recuerdos nos ha dado Jonathan

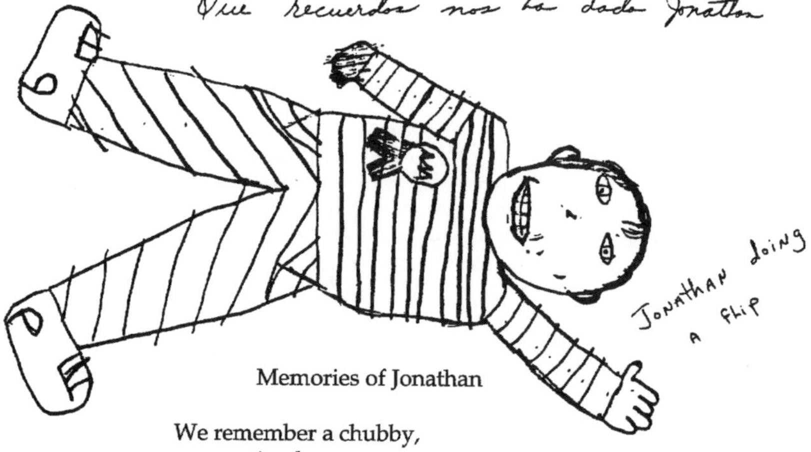


Memories of Jonathan

We remember a chubby,
very active boy
Always looking for mischief to get into
We remember how you cry
when you go to the dentist.
But when you get to his office
you are very brave.
We remember a baby who didn't speak
and now with great pride you speak
both Spanish and English.
What great memories has Jonathan given us.

Because it generates vocabulary and makes timely connections, the acrostic is a particularly useful poetic form, and parents enjoy writing and sharing it. We ask parents to focus on one of their children at a time, and we give them some sample acrostics so they can see how the poetic form works. The rule of the acrostic is that the first letter of each line forms the child's name. This is such a fun nonthreatening way for parents to articulate positive feelings about their children.

We encourage parents to read their acrostics to their children and invite the children to illustrate the poems with their self-portraits. Collections of the illustrated acrostics have become workshop publications. (See Figures 7 and 8 for some examples.)

*ILLUSTRATED POETRY WORKSHOP 2:*
*BIOPOEM/AUTOBIOPOEM*

One problem with prescriptive writing activities is that they soon become boring and overly predictable. Whoever invented the biopoem, however, gave us a pattern that continually renews itself. This pattern is as follows:

Line  1. First name

Line  2. Four traits that describe character

Line  3. Relative ("brother," "sister," "daughter," etc.) of _____

Line  4. Lover of _____ (list three things or people)

Line  5. Who feels _____ (three items)

Line  6. Who needs _____ (three items)

Line  7. Who fears _____ (three items)

Line  8. Who gives _____ (three items)

Line  9. Who would like to see _____ (three items)

Line 10. Resident of _____

Line 11. Last name

When the writer chooses to focus on him- or herself, then the result is an autobiopoem.

In our biopoem workshop, we ask parents to focus on one of their children and to jot down some associations or pictures that come to mind. Individually or in pairs, parents complete the biopoem about the child they have chosen to concentrate on.

FIGURE 7
BEATRICE: ILLUSTRATED ACROSTIC

*Diane Willis/Beatrice Willis*

Beautiful little Being
exciting
a very kind Hearted Person
Terrific
really wants all the attension
is very good with Bady sister
care about all life
eats everything

*FIGURE 8*
*SALVATORE: ILLUSTRATED ACROSTIC*

*Linda Peters/Tore Peters*

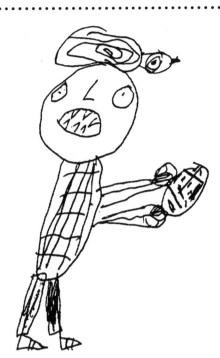

Sensitive to others' Needs
a very caring Person
Leader in and out of School
Very thoughtful boy
an impact player on his Soccer Team

tore is not arrogant nor abusive of others
Oh! he's my son and he's my Gift
really trys in all his endeavors
Eager to learn with a vibrant desire to Progress

Once a draft of the biopoem is completed, participants share aloud in small groups. Each small group then nominates a favorite to be savored by the entire workshop.

The home activity is for parents to read the biopoem to their child. After reading and enjoying the biopoem, the child is invited to create a self-portrait. (Figures 9 and 10 show sample biopoems and illustrations; see pp. 146–148 for blank forms showing the pattern.)

### ILLUSTRATED POETRY WORKSHOP 3: CINQUAIN

There's something about the brevity and symmetry of the cinquain form that continues to fight off the boredom of repetition. The cinquain consists of five lines, and the pattern we suggest is:

Line 1. Child's name

Line 2. Two words that describe your child

Line 3. Three actions or activities you associate with your child

Line 4. A phrase that tells something about your child

Line 5. Either line one repeated, last name, or child's nickname

Like acrostics, cinquains are generally quick in their composition but evocative when real people are being "immortalized." When parents write cinquains about their children, we encourage them to share these poems at home and have their children draw self-portraits. (See Figure 11, and see pp. 149–150 for blank forms and examples.) Collections of illustrated cinquains make for engaging and memorable Parent Project publications.

### SELF-ESTEEM WORKSHOPS

I would say that the number one agenda item for parents today is self-esteem—although it may be termed "attitude," "self-concept," "sense of self," or "self-worth." My own belief is that every aspect of an authentic education enhances self-esteem.

We have found guest speakers such as the school psychologist or social worker to be especially helpful in the self-esteem workshop because they have an informed perspective and can offer parents a

*FIGURE 9*
*JESSICA: A BIOPOEM WITH SELF-PORTRAIT*


*Angela Hudson/Jessica Hudson*

JESSICA
SWEET HELPFUL LOVABLE CARING
SIBLING OF KELLY CAMILLE
LOVER OF JESSIE ANGIE MARGARET
WHO FEELS HAPPY HURT MAD
WHO NEEDS LOVE DADDY MAMA
WHO GIVES PRETTY SMILES LAUGHER TEARS
WHO FEARS DOGS CATS BIRDS
WHO WOULD LIKE TO SEE GREAT GRANDMOTHER GRANDFATHER GREAT GREAT AUNT
RESIDENT OF 1804 N48TH ST
HUDSON

*FIGURE 10*
*RYAN: A BIOPOEM WITH SELF-PORTRAIT*

*Deborah Herbert/Ryan Herbert*

· · · · · · · · · · · · · · · · · · · · · · · · · · · · · · · · · · · · · · · · · · · · · · · · · · · · · · · · · · · · · · · · · · · · · · · · · · · · · · ·

Ryan
Loveable, hyper, caring, helpful
Brother of Michael Jr., Gregory, Daniel
Lover of family, friends, food
Who feels loved, happy, useful
Who needs understanding, respect, space
Who gives love, help, understanding
Who fears darkness, purple, strangers
Who would like to see Mount Rushmore, Batman, Prancer
Resident of Milwaukee, 48th Street
Herbert

*FIGURE 11*
*CINQUAIN WITH SELF-PORTRAIT*

*Blanca Tran/Jimmy Tran*

JIMMY TRAN

Es noble y cariñoso
Piensa, pregunta y admira
Y sus admiraciones son
Un esclamor lleno
De Amor

JIMMY TRAN

He is kind and affectionate
He thinks, asks and wonders
And his wonderings are
An exclamation filled
With Love

number of structures to work with. An enjoyable children's book to read aloud during the guest presentation session is *Willy the Wimp* by Anthony Browne.

Mary Dobbs, La Escuela Fratney's school psychologist, had an especially effective way of beginning the self-esteem workshop. She would go around the circle and ask everyone to tell about something they had done for themselves during the week. (Two of the fifteen parents said "coming to the Parent Project.") Mary's point was that parents who want to encourage self-esteem in their children need to have positive self-esteem themselves.

Another way of starting the workshop is to ask participants to identify something about themselves or their children that they would say is commendable. What are they an "expert" on? (This activity can help identify parents as guest presenters for later workshops.)

Our most successful home activity regarding self-esteem is also one of the simplest. One of the reasons it is so effective is because it contains such a quick reversal on the multiple meaning of language. During the week everyone is to "catch" one or more of their kids doing something good and try to note in their journal what it was and how they reinforced it.

Here's my journal entry on how Hi-Mount parents responded to this "catch your kid doing something good" home activity:

There are nods and laughs as each parent and teacher adds to the "something good" list. There's washing dishes ("I'm not saying they're clean, but they're trying"). There's cleaning rooms ("I was really shocked"). There's reading to a brother, getting good grades, helping with the housework, and taking care of mother when she was sick ("They're big enough now, and now they can take care of me like I can take care of them").

"Stevie, my eight-year-old, just did something phenomenal," one parent begins. "It really made me feel good," begins another.

Angie says she didn't catch any of her kids doing anything good. We talk about it.

## SELF-ESTEEM WORKSHOP 1: BECOMING ME—THE "CHANGE" WORKSHOP
••••••••••••••••••••••••••••••••••••••••••••••••••••••••••

Things happen in Parent Project workshops: to the parents, their children, the teachers, the school, the community. Sometimes these "things" are a direct result of Parent Project workshops; sometimes they are not. Because Parent Project workshops are experiential and participant-driven, we are continually caught up in the process of change. When parents think of their children, they are uplifted when they start to recount how their children have grown over time, and inevitably such discussions start to focus on dreams for their children's future.

One way to enter into this dialogue of change, growth, and dreams of the future is to begin with workshop participants listing and reflecting on major changes in their own lives. We tell them that if life is a stream and there are a series of stepping stones* across this stream and if each stepping stone is an important change in their life, they should try to describe or draw some of these stepping stones in their journal. After a couple of minutes, we have participants envision what the next stepping stone in the stream might be—what they see to be the next major change in their life—and to spend a couple of minutes writing about that. Another activity to follow this one is to ask parents to focus on one child at a time and envision the next "significant change" in that child's life. A follow-up small group discussion could focus on what factors need to be present to support this change.

After discussion about the positive and negative aspects of "change," participants are invited to write and illustrate "Becoming Me," using the forms that appear on pages 151–152. The piece can be about themselves or about one of their children. (Examples are shown in Figures 12 through 14.) Especially when written about their children, the "Becoming Me" pieces tend to define self-esteem. Parents also enjoy seeing how their children complete "Becoming Me" at home. Like the family stories, the cinquain, and the biopoem, "Becoming Me" cries out for publication. Using the "Becoming Me" pieces in small group discussions allows parents to share what factors promote and beget positive change. In the whole group it is interesting to apply these factors to school issues such as grades and evaluation as well as to child-development concerns and self-esteem.

We always try to have book sharing and journal writing as given parts of any workshop structure, and there are numerous children's books that extend and complicate our discussions. An enjoyable choice—especially in the "complicate" category—is *Changes* by Anthony Browne.

The "Change" workshop is a powerful goal-setting and networking experience for all participants. Many layers of the workshop can be pursued and extended in fruitful ways and, as always, group interest and need guide the way.

---

*The "stepping stone" idea comes from Ira Progoff in his book,* At a Journal Workshop.

FIGURE 12
EXAMPLE OF "BECOMING ME" PIECE

*Magalis Johnson/Samuel and Adam Johnson*

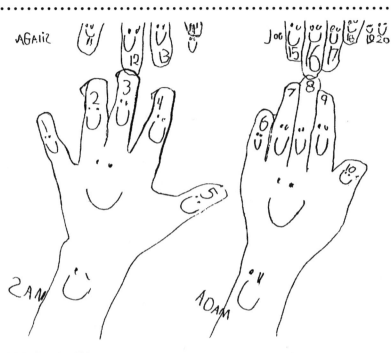

«LLEGARAN A SER»
Samuel y Adam,
una vez eran muy pequeños,
pero ahora son más grandes.
Si se me concediera un
deseo para ellos, este sería,
que ellos fueran.
    buenos muchachos
en el día de mañana.
        Yo se que podrán cambiar
el mundo, si son
            buenos muchachos.
    Una vez ellos no podían
hablar, antes se sentían con
miedo pero ahora saben más
Una vez ellos eran más
tranquilos pero ahora ellos
son más traviesos.
        Magalis Johnson

"THEY WILL BECOME"
Samuel and Adam,
once they were very little,
but now they are older.
If I were to be granted
a wish for them, it would be,
that they can become
        good young men
in the future.
    I know they'll be able to change
the world, if they are
        good young men.
    Once they were not able to speak,
before they used to be
scared to, but now they are more knowledgeable.
Once they were
calmer but they are
more mischievous now.
        Magalis Johnson

*FIGURE 13*
*COMPLETED "BECOMING ME"*

Draw a self portrait

Once I was _Sick_

Now I am _better_

Once I lost _my tigers eye_

But then I found _$5⁰⁰ at the zoo_

If I could have one wish, it would be: _to be a millionare_

If I could change the world, the world would see _Ninja turtle stuff everywhere_

Once I couldn't _walk_

But now you should see me _dance_

I used to feel _scared of the dark_

But now I know _it's nothing but shadows_

The one thing I've learned is _being bad gets you in trouble_

Once I was _a baby_

But now I am _seven_

*FIGURE 14*
*EXAMPLE OF "BECOMING ME" PIECE*

*Lizanne Schulrud/Kristen Schulrud*

The Becoming of You

Once you were totally dependent on others.
But now you are able to do many important things by yourself.
If I could have one wish for you, it would be for you to grow up to
be an artist.
I know you can change the world with your sense of beauty.
Once you couldn't understand jokes
But now you can tell them.
You used to be afraid of the dark
But now you know that you don't need a night light.
Once you were the baby of the family
But now you are a big cousin to Gina.

by Lizanne Schulrud

*Brainstorming* is a lot like freewriting in its insistence on an atmosphere of acceptance and trust. While brainstorming, people shout out (or write) whatever comes to mind regarding the given topic, and it is particularly important to be honest, accepting, and nonjudgmental.

Whole and small group brainstorming sessions are part of almost every workshop—sometimes oral and sometimes written. Parents do want to know what other parents and teachers think, and when the subject involves helping their kids, brainstorming sessions produce immediate results.

In a self-esteem workshop, we tell parents and teachers that a local hospital has published a list titled *101 Ways to Praise Your Child* (See Figure 15). We hold the list up in front of the group and read a few examples: "way to go," "I trust you," "you're important." Brainstorming, we generate our own list, and when the gods, the custodians, and the electricians are with us, we photocopy all the lists to give to participants at the end of the session. If, during the coming days, participants are trying to "catch their kid doing something good," then the lists are especially useful. We also distribute the printed list we held up earlier, and participants enjoy seeing similarities and differences. If we had handed out *101 Ways to Praise Your Child* before we brainstormed, it would have both discouraged and overwhelmed the brainstorming activity.

Brainstorming different ways that parents praise their children's efforts in school is useful and informative for both teachers and parents. One workshop brainstormed the following list:

- Now you've got the idea.
- I like the way you did this.
- Keep up the good work.
- Tell me more about this.
- Let's save this in your good work folder.
- Thanks for bringing this paper home.
- Wow!
- Good answer!
- Terrific!
- Awesome!
- How beautiful!
- I'm impressed.

- Exactly right.
- Much better!
- Look how you've improved.
- Very creative.
- Dad is going to love to read this story.
- Let's send this to Grandma.
- Let's put this one on the refrigerator.
- I can see what you've described.

---

FIGURE 15
*101 WAYS TO PRAISE A CHILD*
*Charter Hospital of Milwaukee*

Wow • Way to Go • Super • You're Special • Outstanding •
Excellent • Great • Good • Neat • Well Done • Remarkable • I
Knew You Could Do It • I'm Proud of You • Fantastic • Super
Star • Nice Work • Looking Good • You're on Top of It •
Beautiful • Now You're Flying • You're Catching On • Now
You've Got It • You're Incredible • Bravo • You're Fantastic •
Hurray For You • You're on Target • You're on Your Way • How
Nice • How Smart • Good Job • That's Incredible • Hot Dog •
Dynamite • You're Beautiful • You're Unique • Nothing Can Stop
You Now • Good for You • I Like You • You're a Winner •
Remarkable Job • Beautiful Work • Spectacular • You're
Spectacular • You're Darling • Your Precious • Great Discovery
• You've Discovered the Secret • You Figured It Out • Fantastic
Job • Hip, Hip Hurray • Bingo • Magnificent • Marvelous •
Terrific • You're Important • Phenomenal • You're Sensational •
Super Work • Creative Job • Super Job • Fantastic Job •
Exceptional Performance • You're a Real Trooper • You Are
Responsible • You Are Exciting • You Learned It Right • What
an Imagination • What a Good Listener • You Are Fun • You're
Growing Up • You Tried Hard • You Care • Beautiful Sharing •
Outstanding Performance • You're a Good Friend • I Trust You
• You're Important • You Mean a Lot to Me • You Make Me
Happy • You Belong • You've Got a Friend • You Make Me
Laugh • You Brighten My Day • I Respect You • You Mean the
World to Me • That's Correct • You're a Joy • You're a Treasure
• You're Wonderful • You're Perfect • Awesome • A+ Job •
You're A-OK My Buddy • You Made My Day • That's The Best •
A BIG HUG • A BIG KISS • Say: I LOVE YOU.

P.S. Remember a smile is worth 1000 words!

A useful follow-up to the praise workshop is for small groups to problem solve how to support children's academic efforts when those efforts have not been entirely successful. Parents are often torn between their desire to nurture and support their children and their belief that teachers expect them to enforce correctness and the "right answer." It is exciting and affirming for parents to hear teachers discuss "error" and "making mistakes" as natural and necessary parts of growing and learning.

It is impossible to disconnect self-esteem issues from school, and the shared vocabulary between teacher and parent is most productive when it supports, encourages, and focuses on the positive.

*P-Q-P: APPLYING PRAISE TO WRITING* • A writing conference strategy used in many classrooms is called P-Q-P. Developed by Bill Lyons (1981), P-Q-P provides a positive and easy-to-remember way of responding to writing. Lyons describes the process as follows:

**P** (PRAISE)     1. What do you **like** about my paper?

**Q** (QUESTION)  2. What **questions** do you have about my paper?

**P** (POLISH)     3. What kinds of **polishing** do you feel my paper needs before it can be published?

In Waukesha, Wisconsin, school teachers adapted Lyon's method for parents in their Parent Project:

RESPONDING TO YOUR CHILD'S WRITING

Revision deals with the content of a piece of writing.

Let your child read you the piece or part of the piece of writing he/she needs help with.

P (praise):   Listen hard for ideas/information.

Summarize what he/she has written.
"I heard you say . . ."
"Your main point is . . ."
"This is what I heard . . ."

Compliment an idea, phrase, sentence . . .
"I liked the part where you . . ."
"I especially enjoyed . . ."
"You made me laugh (cry) when you . . ."

Q (question): To help the child better explain or describe.
"Could you tell me more about . . ."
"What's the most important thing you're trying to say?"
"Can you build on this?"

When revision is done, when the content is complete, then—

P (polish):  Help with grammar, punctuation, spelling after your child has looked for errors first.

> Proofread with your child.
> "There's something missing here . . ."
> "There's a misspelled word in this line."
>
> Reread, having your child try to correct errors. Then, help him/her with those errors missed.

---

## SPECIAL-INTEREST WORKSHOPS

Special-interest workshops have everything to do with the concerns of workshop participants. These concerns are often connected to different aspects of learning in the specific school classroom, such as conferencing, portfolios, critical thinking, and to larger community issues, such as fire safety (see the "Circle of Belief" chapter for a discussion of a fire-safety workshop).

Conducting a special-interest workshop is always an adventure: really an exploration since the "special interest" of participants almost always leads you into uncharted territory with no detailed workshop map to guide you. But if you identify a good guest presenter and trust in the group to help generate the home applications, you'll be pleased with the results. And, as always, a little surprised.

*Alex Bachman*

"How was school today?"
"Okay."
"What did you learn?"
"Nothing."

Parents want to help their children succeed in school, but they are often uncertain about how to talk to their children about what they are learning. Parents are amused and encouraged when they discover teachers, too, sometimes have the same difficulty. Teachers have a name for this talk; they call it "conferencing."

*READING* • We introduce parents to this concept of conferencing by asking them to bring a favorite children's book to the next workshop. The book might be a favorite of their own or of one of their children. Maybe it is a book that they have checked out of the library. A good time to introduce the reading conference is after the library field trip.

When we assemble, we ask each person to introduce themselves by holding up their book and telling us the title. We have a different conferencing question for each parent as they finish, and we invite participants to ask us about the books we brought. There are no right or wrong answers to these conferencing questions. They are meant to support interest and encourage discussion.

- How did you come to choose this book? Did someone recommend it? Had you read it before? Were you intrigued by the title or cover illustration?

- What did you like best about it? What's your favorite part?

- Do you know anything about the author (and/or illustrator)? Have you read any of the author's other books?

- Is the book mainly for enjoyment, or is there something that you learned from reading it? Anything that made you pause and go "Hmmmm . . . Isn't that the truth?"

- Do you remember any characters from the book? What are they like? Do you identify with anyone or any situation in the book?

- If you could be any character in the book, who would you be?

- Would you recommend this book to another parent?

- Why do you think the author wrote this story?

- Is there anything in the book you'd change? Why? What would you do?
- Have you read the book more than once? What made you keep reading?
- Have you talked to anyone else about this book? What did you say?
- Did you feel okay about the book, or did anything give you any trouble?

After we have heard from everyone in the group, we ask participants how they felt about the questions and answers. Such conferencing seems to work best when it is brief and nonjudgmental, when the person asking the questions listens and learns, when the person being questioned listens and learns, and when the reader (parent, child, or teacher) has self-selected the book.

Once we have generated some consensus about the value of conferencing from the whole group, we circulate our list of questions and ask parents to do some conferencing with their children at home. We encourage parents to come up with their own questions and to put ours in a language and/or phrasing that is comfortable in the home.

*WRITING* • The most useful way to introduce the writing conference is through the parents' own writing—and particularly with the piece the parents intend for the final workshop publication. We begin by having parents and teachers introduce themselves by telling us their name and something about their piece for publication. Parents who want to read part or all of the piece are encouraged to do so. Once again, we ask each participant a different writing conference question:

- Is there any more you want to tell us about it?
- How do you feel about it?
- Are you finished? Do you feel it's complete?
- What part do you like best?
- Why did you choose to write about this?
- Did you learn anything from writing this?
- Is this writing important to you? Why?
- Is this different from other things you've written?
- What's your favorite part? Would you read that part or line again?
- Do you need help with anything?
- Did you have any problem writing this? How did you solve this problem or is it still a problem?

- What's the most important thing you want to say?
- Do you have a title? Are you going to use one?
- What do you want people who read this to feel at the end?
- What else do you want to write?

We emphasize that such questions work best when the writer has self-selected the topic and that before using these questions at home parents should first tell their child what specifically they like about the writing the child has shared. By the end of the writing conference workshop, it is clear that conferencing is a learning strategy that operates the same way in all sorts of situations. The keys to conferencing are the nonjudgmental, information-seeking question and the principle that parents, teachers, and children have continual opportunities to learn from one another.

## SPECIAL-INTEREST WORKSHOP 2: CRITICAL THINKING—THE ME TREE

Critical thinking can be encouraged at home in many of the same ways it is encouraged in the classroom: through predicting, problem solving, classifying, hypothesizing, role playing, comparing, imagining, experimenting, observing, interpreting, surveying, and decision making.

In order to demonstrate how critical thinking works, we ask participants to complete a "Me Tree" (see Figure 16). In the branches of the tree are spaces for listing and/or drawing "positive aspects of me seen by others"; in the soil of the treelike roots are spaces for "positive aspects of me seen by me." The Me Tree is a personal and confidential kind of workshop activity in which we assure participants in advance that what they are doing is private and will not be collected or shared unless someone wants to. The Me Tree activity is an effective way to initiate a discussion of how important it is to have the affirmation and support of others.

To get back to critical thinking. As closure for this activity, we ask participants to decide what kind of tree they are. Do they visualize their Me Tree as a mighty oak, an ancient redwood, a newly planted flowering apple, a Christmas tree? This use of analogy, or metaphoric reasoning, simultaneously encourages numerous critical thinking skills.

Soon, participants are constructing their own examples of questions that encourage critical thinking. For example, what picture comes to mind when I say, "Writing is like . . ." or "Reading is like . . ." or "School is like . . ." or "Today, school was like . . ."?

FIGURE 16
THE "ME TREE"

*Positive aspects of "Me" seen by others*

*Positive aspects of "Me" seen by Me*

## SPECIAL-INTEREST WORKSHOP 3: FREEZE! IT'S A CREATIVE DRAMATICS WORKSHOP

Creative dramatics stretches the mind as well as the body. Creative dramatic techniques often involve mime, movement, and verbal expression. Because it supports and increases concentration, communication, self-awareness, awareness of others, cooperation, and self-esteem, creative dramatics is equally productive at home and in the classroom. Some of our favorite creative dramatics have involved the following:

*MIRRORING* • Participants stand facing each other in pairs. One person starts to move, and their partner mirrors their every movement. Switch the mirror roles after a few minutes.

*THE FANTASTIC MACHINE* • Each participant is invited to become part of a large complicated machine. As a functioning part of this machine, each person has a physical motion and a sound, both of which continually repeat. After each person has decided on their motion and sound, the leader starts to connect the parts of the machine together—initially in a line that branches out. Everyone continues their motion and sound until the entire machine is assembled and operating.

*THE MELTING SNOWPERSON* • Tell people with back injuries to sit this one out! All participants stand and pretend that they are snowpeople.

"The sun is just coming up and you are frozen in your snow person positions. . . . Now the sun is climbing in the morning sky, and the snow gradually starts to melt. FREEZE! . . . Now the sun is bright, hot, and overhead in the sky, and the snowpeople are melting even more, and . . . FREEZE!" Stop before anyone falls to the ground.

Somehow, creative dramatics always connect parents with childhood memories that are fantastic and imaginative. After experiencing creative dramatics themselves, participants meet in small groups to discuss ways that they can use creative dramatics at home with children. Parents are encouraged to try one or more of the suggestions during the week with their children and to make note of whether or not they found the technique useful and successful. Figure 17 shows how one parent and her two children used snowperson exercise to create a cinquain poem for the Parent Project publication.

## SPECIAL-INTEREST WORKSHOP 4: WHAT'S A PORTFOLIO FOR?
• • • • • • • • • • • • • • • • • • • • • • • • • • • • • • • • • • • • • • • • • • • •

*"What do you do with all the great work your kids bring home from school?"*

*"I used to take the kids' homework and throw it in the garbage. But this program helped me to realize that I should talk to my children about what they did. Now I save everything they do and put it in little folders and they can look at it. They will ask to see it."*

# FIGURE 17
## A CINQUAIN INSPIRED BY THE SNOWPERSON EXERCISE

*Nancy Maldonado/Anthony and Angel Feliciano*

Angel

Active, Kind
Drawing, Playing, Talking
He has a very kind heart.

Angel.

During a session at the Walloon Institute, Donald Graves suggested that one way to enter into a conversation as well as into an understanding of *portfolio* is to tap into our human need to save things. It is rare to meet anyone who does not keep some kind of collection—be it angels, rocks, beer bottles, photographs, ribbons, or ethnic cookbooks.

The week prior to our portfolio workshop, we ask parents and teachers to tell the whole group what they collect. This telling is always interesting and often reveals an unexpected area of individual expertise. We then ask everyone to bring one item from their collection to our next workshop, and when we reassemble, the opening introductions focus on this item from individual collections. First we ask participants to reflect on the item they selected: Why did they select it? Is it representative of their collection? What makes this item significant, memorable, and special? After this reflection, participants introduce themselves through the item they have brought—saying whatever they want about the specific item and/or their collection.

The lively and surprising discussion of collections that follows provides the context for defining portfolios and how they are used in the classroom. We generally have teachers or children bring in actual portfolios to share with parents, and discussion shifts to issues of ownership and purpose.

In many classrooms, there are two kinds of portfolios:

- a "working" folder that contains all of the students' writing and projects, and
- a "showcase" folder in which certain pieces have been selected for their special significance.

We suggest that parents might want to keep similar kinds of portfolios in the home and that the movement of pieces from the "working" to the "showcase" portfolio offers parents a fine opportunity to affirm their children's achievements.

We ask participants to reflect on how they talked about the items they brought to the workshop from their own collections as a way of showing how important it is for their children to be part of the "showcase" decision-making process.

## CLOSURE/CELEBRATION WORKSHOP: A FINAL DAY IN THE LIFE OF THE PARENT PROJECT

This final workshop is often a community celebration that includes food, children and spouses, school officials, music, raffles, and lots of picture taking. The week before the final workshop, we tell participants that we will begin with everyone's "famous last words." "Famous last words" is one of the closure strategies described by Harvey Daniels and Steve Zemelman in their book *A Writing Project* (1985).

In our "famous last words" each workshop participant gets an opportunity to introduce themselves and any other family members who might be present. Then come the actual "famous last words"—any comment the person wants to make about their experiences in the Parent Project workshops.

Here's my journal record of one such round of closing statements:

*September 12, Hi-Mount School, 4:45 P.M.* Here we are in Marian Catania's fourth-grade classroom again—five years after our first Parent Project workshop. Famous Last Words are in progress:

- "Fun. I really feel good about coming."
- "Helped me and my kids."
- "I like Joan sending those letters to remind me. It is helping me with my children."
- "I like being involved with people focusing on being better parents."
- "I'm glad we have teachers and parents together. It makes me closer to my children and my children with their teachers."
- "For some reason I listen more to my daughter now. Whatever she says that relates to school, I listen. I stop what I'm doing."
- "It helps me see how different school is for my children."
- "I wish my parents had this experience. It would have helped them."
- "Interesting, and it helped me teach my son and bring his grades up by going to the library."
- "He's been doing it (writing) since kindergarten, and now I know what it's like to publish."
- "Just to know the teacher is a plus."
- "It has brought me closer to my children."

After the "famous last words," we distribute copies of the workshop publication. We try to publish enough copies so that all members of each participant's family can have their own. It's important to give everyone enough time to enjoy the publications—to do some autographing and spontaneous sharing. This is a good time to talk about book publishing in the home. (For further discussion on publishing, see the following chapter, "Publication.")

There are a number of logistical things to take care of in this last workshop. Be sure to give parents and teachers the dates for the follow-up workshops. If these haven't been scheduled, then you can ask for help in organizing them, and you might as well take a poll of time and day preferences. What kinds of issues do parents and teachers want these follow-up workshops to address? Here we are, in the midst of the "final" workshop, setting the future agenda.

An effective and appropriate small group discussion topic is what parents and teachers want to accomplish with their children (or an individual child) before the next scheduled follow-up network meeting. This goal setting doesn't work that well, however, if other family members are present since there is a lot of competition for attention (like the potluck dishes of food). If you know what they are going to be, clarify the details of the follow-up workshops: stipends? child care? how will people be notified?

We need some kind of evaluation feedback from everyone before they go. Whatever form we use (see pages 153–156 for sample forms), we try to make certain it is accessible—with copies in the various languages of participants. In completing the evaluations, parents have the options of writing out their comments or saying them to another parent, who acts as a "scribe."

When we are organized and all the school machinery is running, we distribute a list of participant names and phone numbers. As people pack up the remains of the food and head for the door, there is that bittersweet feeling that comes with the end of every workshop. It's a combined sense of being excited and exhausted. Lights out, and don't forget to unplug the coffee.

## RESOURCES:
## ALL OF US

These Parent Project workshops are doable only if you trust that the resources will be found as you develop the need for them. "Parent involvement" describes such an enormous uncharted territory—consider yourself among the true explorers as you feel the occasional accompanying anxieties.

The best resources are those people around you—all of us—each other. Through the guest presentations and the small and large group discussions, the talents of those present emerge and coalesce. Brief handouts, articles, books, and videotapes are very helpful to parents and teachers, but it is often the truths learned through group interaction and discussion that are remembered and acted on.

Clearly, parents are their children's greatest resource, and parent interest in more information and knowledge seems to increase with every workshop. I remember during our first Parent Project workshop at Hi-Mount suddenly realizing that over half of the parents who had dropped out of school had made plans to return for their GED by the end of the first six-week workshop. In his interview with Parent Project participants, Craig Sautter's conversation about career aspirations and the parents' own education went like this:

All of the women returned to school to get their GED or pass the high school equivalence test and have career aspirations toward which they are working.

"I dropped out before tenth grade when I got pregnant with my second child," said Hudson. "But it is so hard without that diploma, so hard. I should have had it a long time ago. But now I am making the effort to get it."

"I finished my high school diploma earlier this year," Robinson revealed. "Suddenly, it became really important to me. And now I really feel good about it. I'm going to continue in school."

The program made a difference in their lives and the lives of their children.

"This program is terrific," said Robinson. "Almost all the little assignments we did involved our kids so it made them feel special. My kids really like it. I learned that I could be a valuable part of my kids' education. That's the main thing. I don't want my kids to be like I was. School is not something you have to endure." (1991)

This, then, is part of the nature of "resource" in our Project—parents as a "valuable" in their children's learning.

Octavio Suncion/Jesse Suncion

Jesse
   Callado expresivo;
   ~~el~~ playing, watching
   thinking.

   I never know, for
   ~~sure~~, what I'm
   thinking about.

Ayorto

Jesse

# Publication

An essential organizing principle of our ongoing workshop structure is the publication of parent/child/teacher collaborative work. We produce these bookletlike publications at the end of each six-week workshop series and at least once a year with the follow-up network.

Our initial reason for publication had to do with the fact that the parents' children were publishing books in their classrooms. We wanted parents to be able to participate in a similar kind of experience and to see how they could publish their own children's books at home. Publication also gave parents a way of knowing and understanding writing workshop and a means of supporting response, revision, and editing in the home.

In retrospect, it is now clear that publication of parent/child/teacher work does much more than familiarize parents with the writing process. Because the publications encourage parents to focus positively on one or more of their children, they formalize and reinforce a positive nurturing dynamic between parent and child as well as serving as a timeless document of the particular parent workshop group and what it accomplished. Not only are these publications fun to do, but they provide a historic marker, a kind of monument to be positive.

Publications take numerous forms—from pop-up books to stories to personal narratives to biographical poems to informal essays. We use whatever bookbinding process is available at the school site—usually a simple spiral binding. (Donald Graves in *Writing: Teachers and Children at Work* has an excellent section on bookbinding, pp. 59–63.)

The key to all publications is that they contain collaborations between parent and child. How this usually works is that parents and teachers generate writing about their child, share this writing with their child at home, and have the child draw a self-portrait. (Teacher participants who do not have children of their own choose a student from their classroom to focus on.) We then publish the collection of illustrated writings and distribute a copy to all members of the parent workshop. Children also receive their own copies of the book, so be sure and print enough.

We initiate the publication by sharing different options with workshop participants in order to gain input about what kind of publication they want. In generating the draft, we encourage a number of options—the principle being always to work within the parent's individual comfort level. Thus, some parents write their draft out longhand, some use computers (when available), some work in pairs, some collaborate with the teacher participants, some tape-record their story for later transcription, and some tell their story to a workshop "scribe."

We try to make publication simple and fun and to involve parents as much as possible in the entire process. Depending on the group and facilities and resources, some published books are handwritten and some in a typed format. Our goal is for the publication to be a celebration of the bond between parents and their children, and we do everything we can to make the publication positive and self-affirming. We are not trying to teach writing, but to give parents access to the process, so we are not concerned about the "correctness" of the final work. We encourage parents to record their stories, poems, and memories in whatever language is most comfortable. We also encourage parents to be positive in writing about their children, and they are. Because they do focus on the positive, the publication enhances the self-esteem of the child as well as the parent, who has now also emerged as an author.

Occasionally, and for a number of reasons, a parent does not complete the piece for publication, and that is fine—our aim is to facilitate, not to judge or grade. Parents who do not complete this piece for publication are, of course, given copies of the book and included in the final workshop celebrations.

When we distribute the publications to the parents and their children, it is a remarkable moment in which the parent's writing becomes their child's reading. From the evaluations over the years, it is clear that publishing is one of the favorite activities of all participants. Once again, it is important to insure that publication in the Parent Project has no punitive aspects to it at all. Publication is a celebration, and parents who don't participate, for whatever reason, are still very welcome at the party.

One of the reasons we want to involve parents as much as possible in actual publication is so that they feel comfortable publishing at home. We demonstrate to parents that publishing their children's writing is easier than it sounds. All they really need to publish their children's writing is something to fasten the pages together; staples, tape, glue, thread, metal rings, paper clips, and even bobby pins have been used in the binding. And to have their children illustrate the cover, tops it off.

Big, small, shaped, illustrated, fiction, fact, autobiography— when parents help publish their children's books at home, it is a time for rejoicing. By its very nature, publishing children's writing enhances everyone's self-esteem and formalizes the connection between reading and writing.

Teachers bring in published books of children's writing from their classrooms to show parents the range of possibilities. Clearly, the cover of the book and the way the pages are bound together will determine how long the book will last in the home library. To make the publishing process more authentic, we suggest that parents and children choose a name for their Family Publishing Company. Some Family Publishing Companies duplicate the actual format of trade children's books, including copyright, title page, and a note about the author. A few blank pages at the end of the book offer future readers a chance to record their reactions—like the responses to Lindsay Claninger's "The Second Grade Bever" shown in Figure 18.

*FIGURE 18*
*RECORDED REACTIONS TO "THE SECOND GRADE BEVER"*

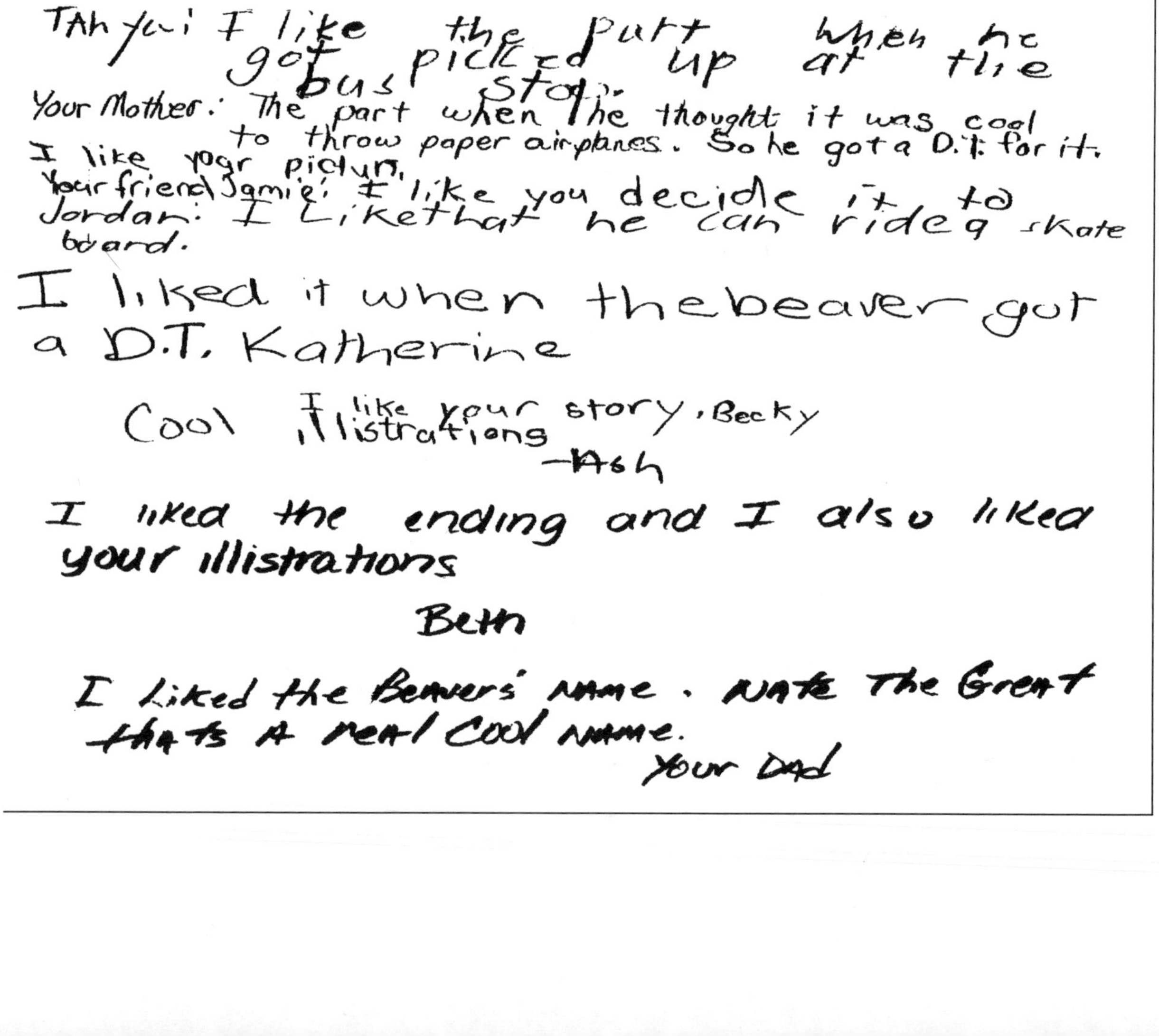

TAh you: I like the part when he got picked up at the bus stop.

Your Mother: The part when he thought it was cool to throw paper airplanes. So he got a D.T. for it.

I like your picture.
Your friend Jamie: I like you decide it to

Jordan: I Like that he can ride a skate board.

I liked it when the beaver got a D.T. Katherine

Cool I like your story. Becky illustrations —Ash

I liked the ending and I also liked your illistrations

Beth

I liked the Beavers name. Nate The Great that's a real cool name.
Your Dad

*Bertha Zamudio*

### LINDOS RECUERDOS DE MIS HIJAS E HIJO

Se me figura, que casi fue ayer,
cuando por primer vez llege a la maternidad,
en sí ya han pasado multiples lunas
convirtiendose en años, llenos de dicha y felicidad.
A través de ese tiempo he visto a mis niñas y mi niño
Xóchitl, Amada y Bernardo creciendo fuertes,
empapados
de la vida, dicha, y prosperidad. Son ellas y él los que me
trasmiten le fuerza para continuar adelante. Luchando
por un
mejor mundo seriamente humano y responsable por
la humanidad y nuestro planeta tierra. Son mis deseos de
que el
día de mañana, ellos vivan un mundo nuevo,
armónico,
cerca a las leyes de la naturaleza. Para que con estas,
evolucionen sa
y no se peirdan en el caos de la
superviviencia,
como lo es en la actualidad.
Que la paz sea con ellos durante el transcurso de sus vidas,
en donde quiera que esten.
Con gran amor maternal, Bertha.


### BEAUTIFUL MEMORIES OF MY DAUGHTERS AND SON

It seems to me that it was almost only yesterday,
when I first arrived at motherhood,
when in reality, many moons have passed
and they have turned into years, filled with joy and happiness.
Throughout this time, I have watched my girls and boy
Xóchilt, Amada, and Bernardo growing strong,
soaked with
life, joy and prosperity. It is they who give me
the strength to forge ahead. Fighting
for a
better world, seriously human and responsible towards
humankind and our planet earth. I wish that
in tomorrow's world, they live in a new world,
harmonious, closer to
the laws of nature. So that with these (laws)
they evolve
and so that they may not get lost in the chaos of
surviving,
as it is in our current world. May peace be with them during the
course of their lives, wherever they may be.
With great
maternal love, Bertha.

*Cynthia Williams/Kenyetta Williams*

*Cynthia Williams/Kenyetta Williams*

## THE BECOMING OF YOU

ONCE YOU WERE . . . . . . . . . .

    AN EMBRYO, THE BEGINING OF LIFE, GROWING INSIDE MY
    STOMACH BECOMING A PART OF ME.

BUT NOW YOU ARE . . . . . . . . . .

    A BEAUTIFUL, ADORABLE, AFFECTIONATE, AND CHARMING
    (7) SEVEN YEARS OLD THAT I LOVE DEARLY.

IF I COULD HAVE ONE WISH FOR YOU, IT WOULD BE . . . . . . . . . .

    FOR YOU NOT TO GET INVOLVED WITH ALL THE BAD THINGS THAT
    ARE GOING ON OUT THERE IN THE WORLD, AND JUST BE THE
    BEST YOU CAN BE.

I KNOW YOU CAN CHANGE THE WORLD WITH YOUR . . . . . . . . . .

    PLEASANTRY, SENSE OF HUMOR, POSITIVE ATTITUDE AND KINDNESS.

ONCE YOU COULDN'T . . . . . . . . . .

    WALK VERY WELL, OR TIE YOUR SHOES OR TALK, YOU JUST
    MADE SOUNDS.

BUT NOW YOU CAN . . . . . . . . . .

    TALK NON-STOP, SPEAK SPANISH, TIE YOUR SHOES, WALK & RUN
    USE THE MICROWAVE, AND A LOT OF OTHER THINGS.

YOU USED TO FEEL . . . . . . . . . .

    THAT THERE WERE THINGS YOU COULD NOT DO.

BUT NOW YOU KNOW . . . . . . . . . .

    THAT YOU CAN DO JUST ABOUT ANYTHING YOU WANT TO DO,
    IF YOU JUST PUT YOUR MIND TO IT.

ONCE YOU WERE . . . . . . . . . .

    AN EMBRYO, THE BEGINING OF LIFE.

BUT NOW YOU ARE . . . . . . . . . .

    MY LITTLE GIRL GROWING UP TO BE AN EXQUISITE, CONSIDERATE
    YOUNG WOMAN.

                              TO KENYETTA WILLIAMS
                              FROM YOUR MOTHER CYNTHIA WILLIAMS
                              WITH LOVE

# Evaluation

Evaluation issues range from parents' questions about how their children are tested and graded to the Project's own need to gauge the success of its workshops and the long-term effectiveness of the workshop approach.

Parents are, naturally, interested in how their children are graded and tested. If the school has begun to use a portfolio approach to evaluation, then surely parents need to be provided access into the definition, use, and significance of the portfolio approach. (See What's a Portfolio For? Workshop, p. 95.) If parents are concerned about their children's standardized test scores, then not only is a guest presentation in order, but also a whole group reading of *First Grade Takes a Test* by Miriam Cohen.

Evaluation of the Parent Project workshops themselves should be ongoing. In the first year of workshops, such evaluation is relatively easy because of the relatively small number of participants. As the program expands, however, evaluation becomes more complex and long term. It is the well being, academic success, and academic persistence of the parents' children that ultimately measures the worth of our parent involvement efforts. Documenting the success of the children is possible but, especially in large bureaucratic school systems, often difficult, erratic, and inconclusive.

It seemed when we began to develop the Parent Project that people wanted evaluation data before we completed the first workshop series. Through the responses of teacher and parent participants, we knew we were being "successful," but the question remained as to how we could communicate this to the general public.

I remember a meeting with Milwaukee Public School Superintendent, Dr. Robert Peterkin, during the first-year development of the Parent Project. The first six-week workshop series had just been completed at Hi-Mount Elementary School, and Dr. Peterkin asked me for evidence that our workshop approach was successful. I looked over the materials I had brought with me, and then handed him a copy of our first Parent Project publication—*The Incredible Illustrated Cinquains.* Dr. Peterkin read through the book with an obvious sense of enjoyment and surprise, and when he returned the book to me, I could tell that he had become convinced. One thing I realized from this experience was that, since we are a workshop program, we have actual results that are persuasive, and one of the most persuasive of all these results is the teacher/parent/child collaborative publications.

At some point during the sixth and last meeting of the initial workshop series, there needs to be some time for parent and teacher participants to reflect on and evaluate the experience. The same holds true for participants in the monthly follow-up network— with such evaluation usually occurring at the end of the school year.

If an evaluation form is used, it needs to be user-friendly and direct, and we have the best results when participants are involved in formulating the questions (see pp. 153–156 for samples of the evaluation forms we have used). We give parents the options of writing, tape-recording, or having another parent transcribe their responses. We also try to insure that the evaluations are available in the languages of all participants. These evaluations give us important information on each parent workshop series, and taken together over time, they allow us to see useful patterns and to set long-term goals.

Another kind of evaluation that began toward the end of our first year of workshops involved letters from parent and teacher participants. Sometimes these letters were addressed to me, or to the cofacilitators of the group; other times the letters were sent to the principal, superintendent, or school board (see "Advocacy" chapter).

Towards the end of the second year of the Parent Project, you are probably going to want to look at the school records of children whose parents have persisted in the program. The data I encountered when I tried this was not very helpful. First of all, the children's "official records" did not contain the same kind of information for each child, and the information that was available was not consistent from school to school or student to student. The only data consistently available was the third-grade standardized reading score, the number of absences, tardiness, and official complaints to the office.

If you need statistical data, and you have similar kinds of difficulties with student records as I did, another kind of statistic to look at is the persistence of the parent/teacher participants. Of those who begin, how many complete the initial six-week workshop? How many continue to participate through the monthly follow-up network meetings? There are so many competing factors for parents' time and attention, and a parent's decision to stop or postpone continued participation in the program is often complicated. Whenever possible, we try to contact "missing" parents in order to understand the context of their decision.

## BUT, DOES IT WORK?

We know the workshop approach to parent involvement works. Perhaps the most persuasive evidence comes out of our experience with the Help Yourself Program in Beloit, Wisconsin. This particular program involved approximately one hundred fourth- to seventh-grade low-income children—all of them African American, Hispanic, or members of another minority group. Although parent participation in the Help Yourself Program was "mandatory," there had been a precipitous decline in such participation from the inauguration of the program in 1988. By the end of 1992, parent participation in the Beloit program had dropped to only 28 percent.

In an attempt to stabilize and perhaps reverse this three-year trend toward noninvolvement, we introduced the Parent Project workshop model at the beginning of the 1992-93 school year. Parent co-facilitators were identified and trained; child care, transportation, and stipends were provided; and lines of communication strengthened. Parents were encouraged to use journals and given increased opportunities for input and ownership.

FIGURE 19
*FAMILY PARTICIPATION RATE AT BELOIT ACADEMY, 1988–1993*

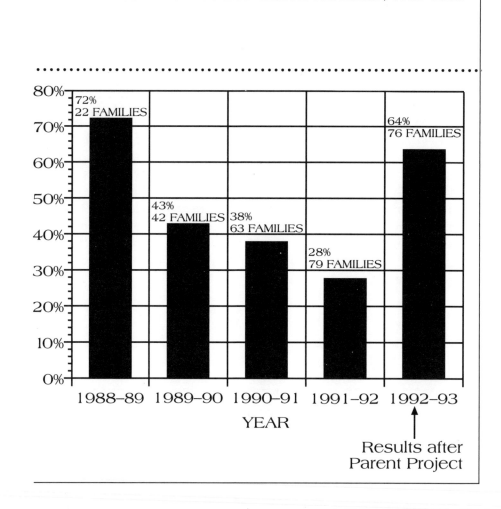

The results were immediate and compelling. (See Figure 19.) By March 1, 92 percent of the parents (seventy-six families) had participated in at least one workshop or event and 64 percent (seventy-six families) were regular weekly participants. By the conclusion of the 1992-93 year, parent involvement had increased 128 percent over the previous year. This meant that the steady three-year decline in parent involvement had not only stabilized—it had dramatically reversed.

And what about the parents' children? The Piers-Harris Self-Concept Scale had been administered to children in the Help Youself Program the year before we began the Parent Project and was given again at the end of our first year, 1992-93. During this period, the self-concept of seventh graders as measured in the "much above average" category increased from 11 percent to 67 percent.

## THE HI-MOUNT STUDY

Another study of the effectiveness of the Parent Project was conducted by Dr. Jerome Blakemore of the University of Wisconsin–Milwaukee. In his study, Dr. Blakemore focused on school suspension rates and behavior problem referrals for children of parents involved in our workshops at Hi-Mount Elementary School. Dr. Blakemore found that there was a 66 percent reduction of school suspensions for children of Project parents and an 82 percent reduction in behavioral problem referrals. In addition, tardiness reports on children of parents involved in the program declined almost 400 percent (from a total of one hundred and ten during the first marking period to twenty-eight during the final marking period).

*Jackie Patterson/Justin Patterson*

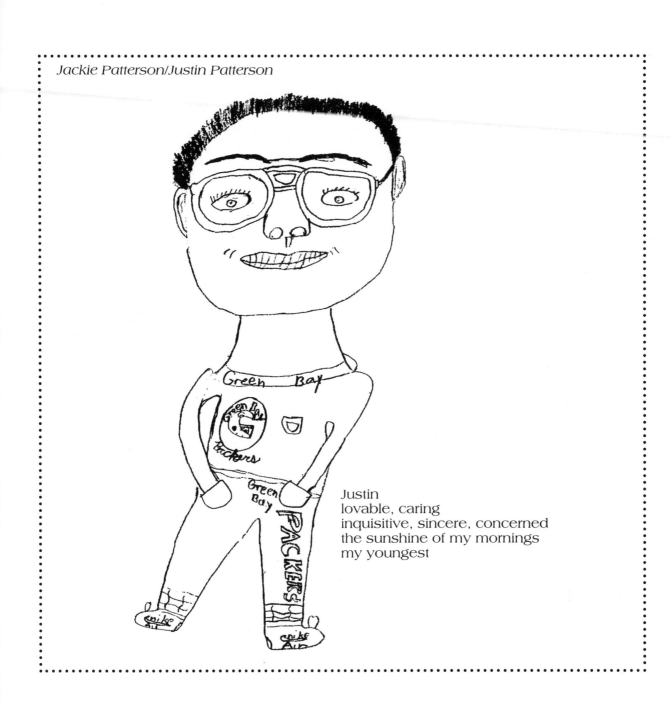

Justin
lovable, caring
inquisitive, sincere, concerned
the sunshine of my mornings
my youngest

# Advocacy

The workshop approach to parent involvement creates advocacy because it not only gives parents access to issues, but also creates this access through a greater awareness of the power, the significance, of individual and collective "voice." It is difficult, if not impossible, for parents to become educational advocates when the basic definition and means to such advocacy is withheld. Our approach to parent advocacy is to demystify the day-to-day school experience while encouraging and supporting the individual and collective voice of parents. As one participant remarked after illustrating a story for her children, "It's not a van Gogh, but it's a Nancy."

In our experience, parents welcome responsibility and accountability. Parents will readily work to guarantee the best education possible for their children. They are, however, frustrated in this desire when the crucial information is withheld, when their good will is diverted into the world of cookie sales and trivial classroom record keeping.

Advocacy takes many forms and actions—involving the parent, child, family, school, community, district, state, nation . . . the world. Our initial purpose in beginning the Parent Project was to connect parents with the classroom curriculum in meaningful ways. We soon learned that the workshop process also increased parent access to the tools of power and the means of advocacy (that is, print, group support, confirmation of voice).

When I think about advocacy, I think of Bonnie Robinson, a parent of two children attending Hi-Mount Elementary School. During the second year of our Parent Project, we were able to arrange a meeting with the Deputy Superintendent for the Milwaukee Public School District, Dr. Deborah McGriff. The workshop group had selected Bonnie to represent them at the meeting, and she had reluctantly agreed to go. The meeting began, and I could feel Bonnie's anxiety. I also noticed that Bonnie had brought her journal. When Dr. McGriff asked Bonnie how she felt about the Parent Project, Bonnie said that she was nervous about the meeting and so she wrote down some of her thoughts in her journal. Bonnie then opened her journal and read for about ten minutes. It was, in its own way, a historic moment for all present.

When I think about advocacy, I think of the individual and collective letters that generate from workshop discussions. Here are the original drafts of two letters written by parents in response to a proposed budgetary cutback in services at Hi-Mount and Sherman Elementary Schools.

To:      Dr. Howard Fuller, Superintendent of the Milwaukee Public Schools
From:   Lela Hightower
Subject: Maintaining Services at Current Level at Sherman and Hi-Mount

I am writing with concern about propose cut In K-4 Program, our kids need that program at that age they are at their best ability to learn. I am a Mother of five and Grandmother of eight, Foster mom of 12.

At Present I have four foster kids In my home, so you see I do have a concern, for I am trying to adopt the four kids I have in my home at present. And please do not increase class size, or cut elementary support.


To:      Dr. Howard Fuller
From:   Deborah Herbert
Subject: Maintaining services at current levels

I'm a part of a parents project funded by the Joyce Foundation. This program is a joint project between Hi-Mount and Sherman Schools. Through these programs we have been able to see more closely the inner works of the school and who makes these things possible. Many Parents do not know that it is just not the teachers who teach in the schools. If It wasn't for the many other people who help the teachers (in many different ways) they would not be able to, so successfully, teach our children.

The thoughts of the school board to cut the K-four program or to take our full time implementors out of our schools would do so much harm it may not be able to be fixed in the future. In my views as a mother with a 4th and a 3rd grader already in school and a four year old (who will hopefully start school next year) and a two year old at home, is that the K-4 program helps the children adapt to a new experience (being in a room full of strangers, without their parents) and get comfortable enough with that that they still can learn and feel comfortable doing it.

Some children can achieve this in a couple of weeks. It takes others longer, but it makes sense to me to have this accomplished before they reach K-5. As for our full time Implementors, they do so much for our students that parents who are not as involved with our schools do not see. If I didn't know what these people did I may not be writing either, but if more parents were informed on what is done you would be reading alot more letters. If the full time implementors are taken out of our schools you probably will be getting even more letters wondering why our schools have lost so much. But these are things that have to be thought about before they happen.

The first step to keeping our kids in school is to get them so interested in school at the grade school level that they don't want to quit. Increasing class size or cutting the people who help so much to make these things happen would be the biggest mistake we could make. Think about the future costs to get these kids reinvolved. It would greatly out weight the cost if we keep the people responsible for keeping our kids involved now.

When I think about advocacy, I think of the many changes we've witnessed over the years with parents and teacher participants. My journal entry from the beginning of a follow-up network meeting at Hi-Mount Elementary School is both individual and representative:

We begin with all of us writing "my news" in our journals followed by individual sharing. Angie's big news is that she is back in school training to be a paralegal through a program at the technical college. Bonnie says that she has completed her G.E.D. equivalent during the summer, and that she is continuing daily writing in her journal. Gloria is now working in a factory with only twenty minutes for lunch and only a ten-minute break in case of emergency. Linda, the kindergarten teacher, has gotten married and everyone applauds. Gloria has also returned to school. Mike has spent the day organizing a parent protest against a proposed cut in the school's Chapter I program. Marian, the fourth-grade teacher, tells Debbie how much Debbie's son, Ryan, is improving. Debbie shares a children's book she has checked out of the library with Ryan. Jim says his back injury is getting worse, but that he still keeps a daily dialogue journal with his daughters, Tina and Mary. Sharon asks about people who are absent. We talk about the children who have been taken away.

One of the things I've learned from my work with the Parent Project is that there are many ways to make a difference.

Rob
Meticulous, Athletic
Wrestles, Collects, Sorts
Animal Lover
Buddy

# Frequently Asked Questions About the Parent Project

Q: Six sessions doesn't seem long enough to have an impact on parents. Is it?

A: Actually, dramatic changes often occur after only a couple of sessions. In one of our early workshops, three parents announced that they were returning to finish school—and this was only our third week. The initial six-session format seems limiting only if it is considered to be an end in itself rather than a beginning. The monthly follow-up workshops allow for ongoing support and change—not only throughout the year, but throughout the years.

Q: Why separate parents from their children during workshop sessions?

A: We've conducted workshops with children present as well, and some sites bring children in towards the ending of the workshop for a closure activity. In general, we've found that parents enjoy the time with other adults, and it is clearly easier to focus attention on the workshop issues if the parents don't also have to relate simultaneously with their children. As one parent stated in his evaluation: "I'm with my kids all day. It's great to have the opportunity to talk with other adults." At the same time, other parents comment on how curious their children are about what we are doing. The final meeting of the initial six-week workshop series is a good time for the whole family to gather, celebrate, and receive their copies of the Parent Project publication.

Q: Does anyone object to the unedited nature of some of the parents' published writings?

A: Yes, but we continue to argue for the individual and collective "voice" of our participants—teachers, parents, and children. We do not judge the writing of parents; we facilitate and celebrate it.

Q: What does a program like this cost?

A: "Less than the cost of one student who drops out of school" is not an entirely facetious answer. The cost really does vary according to need and resources. The major costs occur when the program begins. Once the structure exists and positive word is out in the school community, workshop costs decrease. The major expenses are the stipends for teachers, parents, and facilitators; child care; and materials (including food for breaks). Stipends for the six-session workshop series amount to at least two thousand dollars. This seems like a lot, but if you see it in terms of numbers of people, it is actually quite cost effective. In most instances, the parent we are working with has three or four children. If you consider the total number of parents, children, and teachers, the stipend cost comes out to about thirty dollars per person (fifteen parents, three teachers, two co-leaders, three children for each adult).

*Q:* Do schools always offer stipends?

*A:* No. There are a number of Parent Project sites that do not use stipends. La Casa Esperanza has a raffle at the end of each workshop; and the Chapter 1 Parent Project for the Waukesha schools was very successful without stipends. In relatively affluent school districts, parent stipends are unnecessary.

*Q:* If I wanted to start a Parent Project, where would I get funding?

*A:* If your school has a Chapter 1 program, that would be a good place to start. Documentation of parent involvement is a requirement of Chapter 1 funding. If your school has a business partner, they might want to fund part of the program—or to supply some services. If your school has site-based management, then parent involvement can become a line in the annual budget. It is important to be flexible and to look for possible coalitions. For example, sometimes child care can be taken over by the district's after-school recreation program. Local foundations are increasingly committed to strengthening the bond between school and family. Before you go to the trouble of writing a grant proposal, though, check to see if the foundation gives grants to individual schools.

*Q:* What if there aren't resources to continue to run the initial series of six workshops *and* monthly follow-up network meetings?

*A:* You can't choose between either one because both are necessary and dependent on each other. You can combine them, however. There are numerous advantages of having parents in the initial series of workshops meet with the follow-up network. Just make sure everyone is introduced and that the content of the workshop is new for all participants.

*Q:* Any advice on how to read a children's book aloud to a group of parents who are not fluent in one common language?

*A:* The La Escuela Fratney Parent Project is bilingual. One of the co-leaders would read the book in English, pausing at suitable sections in order for her other co-leader to paraphrase in Spanish. After the paraphrase, we would often ask for predictions in Spanish and English as a way of bringing the group back together and refocusing on the text. The next read-aloud would then be in Spanish with the paraphrase in English.

*Q:* There seems to be a lot of emphasis on writing. Does this reflect what happens in practice?

*A:* A workshop does not, by definition, have to include writing. Except for the piece for the workshop publication, journals are generally used as a way of remembering and focusing through words, pictures, notes. I was, however, impressed by

*frequently asked questions
about the parent project*
......................

128

the enthusiasm parents had for writing—especially when such writing focused on their children. Parents who are uncomfortable with writing nevertheless enjoy telling their stories and seeing them transcribed into print. Except for the workshop designed to generate the piece for publication, journal writing involves a very limited amount of workshop time (five minutes). People, for whatever reason, can use this time to reflect.

*Q:* Do parents and teachers continue to bring their journals to workshops?

*A:* More than I initially expected. I think 50 to 60 percent of parent and teacher participants continue to bring their journals. We always bring along extra paper, pencils, and pens for participants who want to get something down but don't have their journals with them.

*Q:* It sounds like the Parent Project requires a great deal of support from classroom teachers. Support in this case would be the use of the writing process and similar strategies in their classrooms. Wouldn't the program surpass the general classroom in variety, scope, and depth?

*A:* This is not a curriculum, but rather a process. We utilize what we believe to be the most effective and informed ways of engaging individuals in exploring issues of importance to them. The Beloit study (see "Evaluation" chapter) demonstrates the effectiveness of the workshop approach, the process, even when unconnected to the classroom curriculum. It seems obvious, however, that the Parent Project as so defined would greatly enhance any whole language inquiry-based school initiative.

*Q:* Do you ever target a specific grade level for the parent participants?

*A:* *Target* always sounds a little unfriendly to me, but we do generally begin with parents of children in kindergarten and first grade. Researchers say that parent interest is highest when their child begins school for the first time. Most of the kindergarten and first-grade parents we work with have other children in higher grades in the school, and so the workshop benefits multiply. A further argument for starting with K-1 parents is that (theoretically) their children will be in the school system the longest.

*Q:* Does everyone do the home activities during the week?

*A:* No, but participation is usually around 80 percent. It's fine for parents to "pass" as we go around for the home activity check-in. Usually everyone does have some observation about their children and schools to share, if not specific to the focus activity. The bottom line is we want all participants in our workshop to have a positive experience. We are not grading participants.

Q: I think many parents would not participate in a program of this magnitude. The level of commitment is similar to that required in a community-college-level class.

A: In general, I have found that people (teachers and parents) don't mind the time spent if they gain something real from it. In many ways we have the luxury of not being a "class." We don't give grades; we don't have a final exam. This forces us to do something relevant every time we meet. Ownership of the agenda by workshop participants is a crucial factor in their commitment to the Project.

*Bonnie Messling/Craig Messling*

Cheerful & happy

Reads books

Asks lots of questions

Interested in school

Good at causing trouble with little sister.

# RESOURCES

# Organization
# and
# Administration

___ Reminder sent to all participants confirming workshop dates, time, and place.

___ Speaking of "place," do you need a Building Permit?

___ If you need a Building Permit, then you probably also need to clear things with the Building Engineer.

___ Agreement or commitment forms. Other attempts to make participants feel "invited."

___ Phone reminders to participants and guest speaker.

___ Food and drinks for Break. Who is setting up?

___ Guest presenters—do they need any special equipment?

___ Child care—including place, personnel, snacks, and materials.

___ Security concerns for workshops held after school and in the evening.

___ Attendance sheet of some sort if paying stipends. (Passing a sheet of paper around and having people "sign in" is still the best.)

___ There is shared responsibility. No one person should try to be responsible for all these items.

## SAMPLE PARENT PROJECT AGREEMENT FORM

To:

From:

❏ **YES,** I will attend the six sessions of the parenting class.

These sessions are scheduled on the following Mondays from 4:00 P.M. to 6:00 P.M.

**NOVEMBER 6TH, 13TH, 20TH, & 27TH, DECEMBER 4TH & 11TH**

I understand that baby-sitting will be provided. I also understand that I will be paid one hundred dollars for my participation in all six classes.

❏ **NO,** I am unable to attend these classes at this time.

❏ Please contact me when you plan to start another session.

YOUR SIGNATURE _____
PLEASE PRINT YOUR NAME _____
ADDRESS _____ ZIP CODE _____
YOUR PHONE NUMBER _____
WILL CHILD CARE BE NEEDED?
IF SO, HOW MANY CHILDREN AND WHAT ARE THEIR AGES? _____

Dear Parents,

Some parents in the Parent Project expressed an interest in learning more about computers; therefore, we are offering a beginning computer class for parents starting Monday, February 10th, from 4:00 P.M. to 6:00 P.M. We will always begin *promptly at 4:00 P.M.* so that we are able to make the best use of our time together.

Our classes will occur as follows:

**Monday, February 10**     **Monday, February 17**
**Monday, March 2**         **Thursday, March 5**
**Thursday, March 12**      **Monday, March 16**

*Child care will be available. Classes will be held in room _____ at _____ School.*

We are looking for parents that are interested in a full six-week commitment to the project. If you are interested in joining us, please return this sheet to the above address by Thursday, February 6th.

❏ I will be able to attend on a weekly basis and will be available at 4:00 P.M.

❏ I will not be available to attend, but please keep my name on the list for future classes.

NAME _____
ADDRESS _____
ZIP _____
PHONE _____
BEST TIME TO CALL _____

## SIGN-IN SHEET FOR THE PARENT PROJECT

| NAME | DATE | TIME |
|------|------|------|
|  |  |  |
|  |  |  |
|  |  |  |
|  |  |  |
|  |  |  |
|  |  |  |
|  |  |  |
|  |  |  |
|  |  |  |
|  |  |  |
|  |  |  |
|  |  |  |
|  |  |  |
|  |  |  |
|  |  |  |
|  |  |  |
|  |  |  |
|  |  |  |
|  |  |  |
|  |  |  |
|  |  |  |
|  |  |  |
|  |  |  |
|  |  |  |
|  |  |  |
|  |  |  |
|  |  |  |
|  |  |  |
|  |  |  |
|  |  |  |
|  |  |  |
|  |  |  |
|  |  |  |

# SAMPLE RECORD SHEET FOR STIPEND PAYMENT

| CHILD | TELEPHONE | ROOM | FIRST NAME | LAST NAME | DAYS PRESENT | | | | | | | | | |
|---|---|---|---|---|---|---|---|---|---|---|---|---|---|---|
| | | | | | | | | | | | | | | |
| | | | | | | | | | | | | | | |
| | | | | | | | | | | | | | | |
| | | | | | | | | | | | | | | |
| | | | | | | | | | | | | | | |

Dear _____ ,

WELCOME to the _____ Parent Project. As you know, we plan to meet in the school library on Thursday evenings from 6:30 P.M. to 8:30 P.M.

*OCTOBER 1ST, 8TH, 15TH, AND 22ND*
*NOVEMBER 5TH AND 12TH*

The purpose of the Parent Project is to inform you of new educational philosophies and how they relate to home and classroom activities. Tentative topics include:

| | |
|---|---|
| October 1 | What's new in education? Interviews, journals, and whole language |
| October 8 | Reading—at home and school |
| October 15 | Writing—at home and school |
| October 22 | Self-esteem—at home and school |
| November 5 | Making a book |
| November 12 | Evaluation, grades, and portfolios |

We will make every effort *to do* activities when we meet as a way of enjoying ourselves and promoting understanding and discussion.

Child care will be in Room 113. We look forward to seeing you next Thursday evening at 6:30 P.M.

## SAMPLE FOLLOW-UP NETWORK LETTER

To:     Parents in Parent Project who completed initial six-week course

From:

Re:     Schedule for Semester II

Please reserve the following dates for the Parent Meetings:

> *Monday, February 4th*
> *Tuesday, March 5th*
> *Monday, April 8th*
> *Monday, May 6th*

All classes will begin in Room 20. The time will be from 4:00 P.M. to 6:00 P.M.

The Parent Project staff got together to plan programs that we feel will meet the needs that you identified for us. We are looking forward to meeting with you on these dates. We ask that you please make *every* effort to be on time. You will be paid for your participation as in the past. In fairness to everyone involved, payments will be adjusted according to the time actually spent in the class. If you can't make a class, please call _____ at school, or leave a message for her.

Thanks for your continued participation. We are looking forward to working together with you for the benefit of the children.

Playful
Respectful
Independent
Sassy
Caring
Inteligent
Loving
Loyal
Argumentive
At time

Priscilla

Rilly

Christmas Day

Age. 8.

# Workshop
## Materials

# THE BIOPOEM/AUTOBIOPOEM

The biopoem follows this general pattern:

Line 1:  (First name of the person the poem is about)

_____

Line 2:  (Four traits of the person's character)

_____, _____, _____, _____

Line 3:  Relative (like "sister," "son," "granddaughter") of _____.

Line 4:  Lover of (list three ideas, things, or people)_____

_____

Line 5:  Who feels (list three items) _____

_____

Line 6:  Who needs (list three items) _____

_____

Line 7:  Who fears (list three items) _____

_____

Line 8:  Who gives (list three items) _____

_____

Line 9:  Who would like to see (list three items) _____

_____

Line 10: Resident of (street? city? state? country? era?—choose one) _____

Line 11: (Last name) _____

In the autobiopoem the writer becomes the subject:

Line 1:   (Your first name) _____

Line 2:   (Four traits that describe you)

          _____, _____, _____, _____

Line 3:   Relative (like "sister," "son," "granddaughter") of _____

Line 4:   Lover of (list three ideas, things, or people)_____

          _____

Line 5:   Who feels (list three items) _____

          _____

Line 6:   Who needs (list three items) _____

          _____

Line 7:   Who fears (list three items) _____

          _____

Line 8:   Who gives (list three items) _____

          _____

Line 9:   Who would like to see (list three items) _____

          _____

Line 10: Resident of (street? city? state? country? era?—choose one) _____

Line 11: (Your last name) _____

La poesía autobiográfica sigue el siguiente patrón:

Línea 1:  Escriba el nombre propio de la persona a la que se refiere el poema.

_____

Línea 2:  Escriba cuatro características que describen a la persona.

_____, _____, _____, _____

Línea 3:  Pariente de/ emparentado con (por ejemplo: "hermana (o)," "hijo (a)," nieto (a))

_____

Línea 4:  Enamorado (a) de (mencione tres ideas, cosas o personas) _____

_____

Línea 5:  Quien siente (mencione tres sentimientos) _____

_____

Línea 6:  Quien necesita (mencione tres cosas) _____

_____

Línea 7:  Quien siente temor por (mencione tres cosas) _____

_____

Línea 8:  Quien da (mencione tres cosas) _____

_____

Línea 9:  A quien le gustaría ver (mencione tres cosas o personas) _____

_____

Línea 10: Residente de (¿calle? ¿ciudad? ¿estado? ¿país?)_____

Línea 11: Apellido (s) _____

_____

*THE CINQUAIN*

Line 1.  Child's name

_____

Line 2.  Two words that describe your child

_____

Line 3.  Three actions or activities you associate with your child

_____

Line 4.  A phrase that tells something about your child

_____

Line 5.  Either line 1 repeated, last name, or child's nickname

_____

Example:

AMY
SENSITIVE HAPPY
HELPFUL KIND GOOD NATURE
MISS HER IF SHE WASN'T HERE.
AMY

Línea 1.   Nombre del niño (a)

_____

Línea 2.   Dos palabras que describen a su hijo (a)

_____

Línea 3.   Tres acciones o actividades que usted asocia con su hijo (a)

_____

Línea 4.   Una frase que expresa algo acerca de su hijo (a)

_____

Línea 5.   Aquí podría repetir la línea 1, el apellido, o el apodo del niño (a)

_____

## Orlando

Orlando:
Inquisitive, bright
Wonders, thinks, asks
Everything he says is followed
by an exclamation mark!

Orlando:
curioso, inteligente
admira, piensa, pregunta
¡Todo lo que dice es una exclamación!

(Draw self-portrait)

Once I was _____ ,

Now I am _____ .

Once I lost _____ ,

But then I found _____ .

If I could have one wish, it would be: _____ .

If I could change the world, the world would see: _____ .

Once I couldn't _____ ,

But now you should see me _____ .

I used to feel _____ ,

But now I know _____ .

The one thing I've learned is: _____ .

Once I was _____ ,

But now I am _____ .

The following is a variation on "Becoming Me."

## The Becoming of You

Once you were _____.

Now you are_____.

If I could have one wish for you, it would be _____.

I know you can change the world with your _____.

Once you couldn't_____,

But now you can _____.

You used to feel_____,

But now you know _____.

Once you were _____,

But now you are _____.

## "Llegaras a Ser . . ."

Una vez tu eras _____.

Ahora sientes _____.

Si se me concediera un deseo para ti, este seria _____.

Yo se que tu puedes cambiar el mundo con tu _____.

Una vez tu no podias_____,

Pero ahora puedes_____.

Antes sentias_____,

Fero ahora sabes _____.

Una vez tu eras _____,

Pero ahora eres _____.

## PARENT PROJECT EVALUATION #1

1. My general reaction to the Parent Project is:

2. I would rate each of our activities (5=highest rating, 1=lowest):

   Using my journal _____
   Meeting and working with other parents _____
   Getting to know the teachers better _____
   Writing with my child _____
   Reading with my child _____
   Guest presentations _____
   Group discussions _____
   Publishing the Parent Project book _____
   Other (please name) _____

3. I think the workshops could be improved if:

4. As a result of these workshops, I want to:

5. Some workshops and activities I wish had been part of the Parent Project are:

6. My final comment on this experience is:

1. People ask how we know the Parent Project is effective. How would you answer, and what specific things would you point to (either in terms of yourself, your children, or school):

2. What should we change about the way the Parent Project operates?

3. Do you have any ideas about how you want the Project to operate next year?

4. Anything else?

1.  Su opinión sobre el proyecto _____

2.  Valore las siguientes actividades, (5 lo más alto 1 lo más bajo)

    Escribiendo mi propio reporte _____
    Conociendo mejor a los otros padres _____
    Conociendo a los maestros mejor _____
    Leyendo a mi niño (o) _____
    yendo a la biblioteca _____
    Presentaciones formales _____
    Usando la computadora _____
    Otros (sea específico) _____

3.  Comentarios de los líderes del grupo

4.  Algunos inconvenientes/frustraciones en las reuniones. Lo que me gustaría que se llevaría a cabo después de ésta reunión

5.  Lo que me gustaría que se llevará a cabo después de ésta reunión

1. What did you like about this project?

2. What would you do differently?

3. What did you expect that didn't happen?

4. What did you try that you hadn't done before?

5. How would you rate this project? CIRCLE ONE:

| 1 | 2 | 3 | 4 | 5 |
|---|---|---|---|---|
| Poor | Not Helpful | OK | Good | Terrific |

Average Evaluation = 4.64

*Alice Warr/Amanda Warr*

The Becoming of you AMANDA

ONCE YOU WERE A SHY LITTLE GIRL
BUT NOW YOU ARE    VERY INQUISITIVE
AND IF I HAD ONE WISH FOR YOU, IT WOULD BE FOR YOU  TO
BE HEALTHY, HAPPY AND SUCCESSFUL .
ONCE YOU  COULDN'T READ OR WRITE
BUT NOW YOU CAN BOOK NUMBERS WITHOUT PEN OR PENCIL
YOU USED TO SOMETIMES FEEL SHY AND INCAPABLE.
BUT NOW YOU KNOW YOUR ABILITIES AND HOW TO USE
THEM IN THE MOST POSITIVE WAYS IMAGINED.
ONCE YOU WERE JUST A BABY
BUT NOW YOU ARE MAMA'S BIG GIRL!!!

by your mother Alice Warr

# Read On—
# The Best
# Endings
# Are
# Beginnings

At almost every workshop, either a parent or a teacher brings in some valuable information to share with the other participants. Sometimes these resources are told to us, and sometimes they are in print and need to be duplicated for distribution at the next meeting.

One of the many things I've learned is that I only become receptive to information once I have a need for it. It was only after we had begun the Parent Project, for example, that I realized every Thursday *The New York Times* contains a "Parent & Child" column devoted to contemporary issues, such as what your daughter can do if she is sexually harassed at school ("keep a written record").

I think every public school district in America has quite an array of information to share with parents; it's just that they often can't seem to find a way to get the information into the hands of parents who need it. "10 Quick Ways to Analyze Children's Books for Racism and Sexism" ("#1. Check the Illustrations") published by the Milwaukee Public Schools is just one example of useful information accessible to parents. The Waukesha Public Schools Chapter 1 Program has a series of pamphlets containing practical suggestions for parents—"Practice estimation with your child. On a trip to the grocery store ask your child to estimate how much the groceries in the cart will cost."

The National Council of Teachers of English (NCTE) publishes "Como Ayudarle a su Niño a Escribir Mejor" ("How to Help Your Child to Write Better"), which contains suggestions of things to do at home and school. Two of the at-home suggestions we found parents most interested in were: "Provide a suitable place for children to write," and "Encourage the child to write for information, free samples, and travel brochures."

County Mental Health Associations will have some information on self-esteem. Once again, much of the advice for parents has to do with being a "positive role model." The National Association of School Psychologists publishes an excellent series of pamphlets regarding such issues as "Children and Responsibility," "Children and Drug Abuse," "Children and Reactions to Death," "Children and Moving," and "Children and Responses to Disaster."

One of the themes that almost all of the resources come back to again and again is how influential the parent example is. Children imitate their parents. "Let your child see what you want them to do" is at the heart of the matter.

The information is definitely out there, and it is really quite consistent in its overall message. The consensus seems to be that these conditions make a home for learning:

**CHOICE.** Children should be encouraged to read the books they want to read, write the stories they want to write. Choice motivates active (rather than passive) learning.

**PRAISE.** "Put ups" instead of "put downs" are basic to learning.

**PREDICTABILITY.** Bedtime stories. Saturday morning family journal time. Regular scheduling provides a sense of value, security, and continuity.

**EXAMPLE.** Children imitate their parents, and so it is important for children to see their parents write, draw, read, keep a journal, go to the library, balance their checkbook, check the calendar, measure ingredients, and use maps to find where they are going.

**PATIENCE.** Learning is not a straight upward line on a graph, but a series of peaks, plateaus, and valleys.

**FUN.** Learning and literacy activities are often playful and spontaneous—done as much for enjoyment as for achievement.

**ACCEPT.** Children need their parents to keep and display their learning.

**SHARE.** Life is learning, and it is usually more fun together. It is important for parents to be part of their children's learning, and for children to be part of their parents' learning. Let's all count change together.

---

## CHILDREN'S BOOKS

---

Children's books, with their wealth of imaginative experience and illustration, offer a rich and enduring resource for our workshops. The following books have proven to be particularly popular in workshops:

Fernando Alonso. *El Viejo Reloj*. España: Unigraf S.A. ALFAGUARA, 1988.*

*Este libro muestra como la exploración, la creatividad y el tesón logran alcanzar un significado en relación a algo inanimado. Habiéndose trazado como meta el encontrar los números del reloj, llevó a este niño a conseguir el resultado deseado en diferentes formas y usos. Su investigación le hizo ver que los números no son solamente signos, sino que ellos también son utilizados en muchas otras formas. El resultado que la imaginación y la creatividad trabajen más.*

*Respecto a la individualidad de los números, el niño piensa y crea sus propios diseños para reemplazar los números desaparecidos del reloj.*

*Esta historia crea un ambiente multiforme en lo educacional. Ayuda a crear, a investigar, y a reconocer los números como tales, y el uso de ellos.*

Keith Baker. *Who Is the Beast?* New York: Harcourt Brace Jovanovich, 1990.

*This is an existential Big Book in which we all discover that the enemy is "us." The size of the book gives the reader a sense that they are walking into the jungle as the simple story is told. Most parents have never seen a Big Book. After enjoying this one, everyone wants to know where to get some more.*

Eduardo Robles Boza. *La Computadora "K-J."* México D.F.: Editorial Trillas.

*La técnica empleada en describir la caja K-J simplemente explica las intenciones de aprendizaje. Los métodos empleados y la realización del objectivo, aunque simple, presenta una disposción firme.*

*Puede tomarse como ejemplo de la tenacidad y de los resultados positivos, especialmente para mentes jovenes en formación.*

*Toma prioridad lo primero, pero existe la potencialidad de la amistad y del propósito.*

*Ejemplo valioso de como empezar un proyecto satisfactorio. Para cualquier grado. Ayuda a lo imaginativo y es constructivo en susmorale jas.*

Anthony Browne. *Changes*. New York: Alfred A. Knopf, 1990.

*On a Thursday morning at 10:15, Joseph Kaye starts to hallucinate—or is the tea kettle really turning into a cat? Joseph's father has told him "things are going to change," and Joseph's imagination takes care of the rest. The surprise at the book's conclusion has a lot to do with definitions of family and love. This book demands to be read at the Change Workshop (see p. 82).*

---

*Annotations of books written in Spanish were prepared by Bertha Zamudio, La Escuela Fratney.*

Anthony Browne. *Piggybook*. New York: Alfred A. Knopf, 1986.

*Mrs. Piggott gets fed up with her male-chauvinist husband and sons and leaves them to wallow in their own domestic mire. With its detailed and satiric illustrations, this book readily raises issues concerning male and female stereotypes as well as the changing role of "wife."*

Anthony Browne. *Willy the Wimp*. New York: Alfred A. Knopf, 1984.

*The suburban gorillas start picking on Willy, but he begins lifting weights and it looks for a time like our hero will emerge unscathed. But of course not, for we are in Anthony Browne's surreal world of reversals. This is a good book to read aloud as part of any self-esteem workshop because it explores the consequences of mental attitude in a comic and meaningful way.*

Eve Bunting. *The Wednesday Surprise*. New York: Clarion, 1989.

*On Wednesday evenings, Anna and her grandmother read stories together out loud as they prepare a surprise for Dad and the reader. The book explores concepts of literacy and reverses a lot of expectations concerning the nature of learning. The working-class setting of the book adds realism and poignancy.*

María Charet. *El Conejo de Chocolate*. Provelica 101—Barcelona 29: Editorial Juventud, S.A., 1983.

*Sin ir demasiado lejos, la pequeña distracción de Pedrito Conejo lleva a su papá a crear sabrosos y mentados chocolates de Pascua.*

*Las ilustraciones, que de por sí son explícitas, dan un buen reconocimiento a la animación de este cuento.*

*Puede dar ejemplos comunes y soluciones satisfactorias a los estudiantes. La simplicidad de su contenido puede tener semejanzas con la vida real—la vida diaria—en cuanto a las emociones, la realización familiar y el modelo familiar.*

Miriam Cohen. *First Grade Takes a Test*. New York: Dell, 1980.

*Standardized testing is dealt a severe blow in this story told from the point of view of multiethnic first graders as they try to make sense of "filling in the box next to the right answer." The book successfully explores the consequences of what it means to be labeled "smart" and "dumb."*

Crescent Dragonwagon. *Home Place*. New York: Macmillan, 1993.

*A family of Sunday hikers come upon the remains of a house in the woods. These artifacts of the past begin to trigger images of the family that once lived*

*read on—the best
endings are beginnings*
. . . . . . . . . . . . . . . . . . . . . .

*166*

in the house. The book is quite mysterious in the way it evokes the past and
generally causes readers to reflect on their own family history and artifacts.

Benjamín Elkin. *Seis Pescadores Disparatados*. Chicago: Children's
Press, 1982.

*La ingenuidad de la historia nos ayuda a relajar la imaginación. El conteo
simple para principiantes en los grados bajos es muy obvio.*
    *El tema ayuda al estudio de las matemáticas simples y a la lógica de
reconocimiento por deducción. El texto muestra también diferentes lugares
o puntos estratégicos de aprendizaje para grados bajos con conteo y comici-
dad. El agradecimiento por la simple deducción y la simpleza de sus carac-
teres dan como resultado una divertida historia ilustrativa de hermandad y
preocupación.*

Guillermo Solano Flores. *La Noche*. México, D.F.: Editorial Trillas,
1985.

*Es un pequeño relato acerca de la noche que acontece durante las horas de
obscuridad. En este cuento el autor da detalles de la vida nocturna de ciertos
animales, de las actividades que llevan a cabo, y de otros pormenores tales
como la vida inanimada de los juguetes y la tranquilidad de las calles.*

Mem Fox. *Wilfred Gordon McDonald Partridge*. New York: Kane
Miller, 1985.

*Wilfred Gordon McDonald Partridge explores the concept of memory with
individuals who live in an "old people's home" next door. The book raises
issues surrounding aging and the illusive nature of memory. Like* The
Wednesday Surprise, *this book also defines the special relationship
between the old and young.*

Debra Frasier. *On the Day You Were Born*. New York: Harcourt Brace
Jovanovich, 1991.

*Moon, tides, animals, and the various forces of nature rejoice in the day you
were born. The epilogue of this book contains a section entitled "More
About the World Around You," which further explores the natural concepts
("spinning earth," "migrating animals," "pulling gravity") mentioned in
the primary text.*

Fiona French. *Snow White in New York*. Toronto: Oxford University
Press, 1990.

*Snow White finds work as a jazz singer in this retelling of the classic fairy
tale. The possibilities for recasting traditional fairy tales in modern urban
settings become readily apparent as you read this book.*

Carmen Garza. *Family Pictures (Cuadros de Familia)*. San Francisco: Children's Book Press.

*Las ilustraciones y el contenido de esta historia tienen gran importancia en lo cultural y en lo personal. Cabe decir que las ilustraciones dan una idea de la vida cotidiana, de las costumbres de un pueblo, de una familia y de una artista.*

*La simplicidad y el realismo de las ilustraciones es lo más significativo pues, de una manera bien detallada, se pueden reconocer los momentos, los lugares y las escenas cotidianas que no necesitan palabras para ser descritas.*

*Es muy realista, simple y da una gran satisfacción emprender el viaje con tanta belleza. Para cualquier edad y gusto.*

*Muestra con detallada precisión los quehaceres domésticos diarios, la vida común cotidiana, las costumbres de los personajes y los sueños por alcanzar metas que se logran con una imaginación muy rica, y con una vehemencia natural.*

*Se recomienda para todas las edades, especialmente para principiantes. Soberbio, único.*

Patricia Reilly Giff. *Today Was a Terrible Day*. New York: Viking, 1980.

*Ronald Morgan has one of those days in second grade in which everything goes wrong. The book contains an effective satire of reading groups and the frustrations that can be inherent in school learning. (See Reading Workshop 3, p. 67).*

Graham Greene. *El Pequeño Tren*. Madrid: Traducido por Franciso Pavon Torres, 1989.

*La historia trata de un pequeño tren aburrido de su rol en un pueblito donde los habitantes dependen mucho de él.*

*La salida es un escape, una aventura para romper con la monotonía.*

*El tren insiste en salir y se encuentra con un mundo grande, desconocido y peligroso. La moraleja de la historia muestra lo que puede suceder al no estar bien preparado y también demuestra el arrepentimiento.*

*Muestra la demografía muy bien ilustrada con montañas y ciudades. Además, incluye el mapa del viaje de la locomotora, el cual puede ser de gran valor en la enseñanza de los estudiantes para leer direcciones. El itinerario simple de esta figura y los momentos que preceden al viaje son explícitos y obtienen la atención deseada. Mediante el uso de moralejas y significados de sus momentos, se crea una atmósfera de duda. Por lo tanto, ayuda educacionalmente a programar, a discernir, y a pensar antes de actuar. Muchas veces lo monótono bien encaminado lleva a caminos inesperados pero seguros.*

Barbara Shook Hazen. *Tiempos Duros/Tight Times*. New York: Penguin, 1983.

*A loving family endures in spite of economic hardships. The black-and-white illustrations by Trina Schart Hyman convey the social realism of the urban setting. In this book it is "scary" but okay for fathers to cry.*

Gloria Houston. *My Great-Aunt Arizona*. New York: HarperCollins, 1992.

*Set in the Blue Ridge Mountains, the book explores the stages of great-aunt Arizona's life, the power of reading, and the enduring presence of a sensitive, caring teacher. Family history and the motivation for becoming a teacher combine in a joyous way.*

Angela Johnson. *Do Like Kyla*. New York: Orchard Books, 1990.

*A day in the life of two sisters told from the point of view of the youngest. The book depicts the tender and caring relationship between the two sisters and subtly reveals how there can be learning and love in everyday occurrences.*

Angela Johnson. *When I Am Old With You*. New York: Orchard Books, 1990.

*An African-American child and his grandfather explore the concepts of memory, history, age, and love across generations.*

Angela Johnson. *Tell Me a Story, Mama*. New York: Orchard Books, 1989.

*Family history, growing up, and moving away are explored through the "family story." The book powerfully illustrates the fact that the stories children hold most dear are those the parents tell of their own life. What are your stories, and when was the last time you shared them with your children? (See I Remember: A Storytelling Workshop, p. 70).*

Jacob Lawrence. *The Great Migration*. New York: HarperCollins, 1992.

*A chronicle of African-American strength, courage, and triumph told through a narrative sequence of sixty paintings. "Around the time I was born, many African-Americans from the South left home and traveled to cities in the North in search of a better life. My family was part of this great migration" (p. 1).*

Arnold Lobel. *Fables*. New York: Harper & Row, 1980.

*The ancient genre of the fable gains some modern satiric twists. The moral of "The Bad Kangaroo" is: "A child's conduct will reflect the ways of his parents."*

Morag Loh. *Tucking Mommy In.* New York: Orchard Books, 1987.

*A wonderful role reversal in which Sue and Jenny tell their tired and overworked mother a bedtime story and tuck her into bed. This is a good book to use in connection with the "catch your child doing something good" home activity from the Self-Esteem Workshop, p. 82).*

Robert Munsch. *Love You Forever.* Willowdale, Ontario: Firefly Books, 1986.

*A story of growing up and how parents' love for their children endures through generations. Bring a box of tissue when you read this book to the whole group—not only will your listeners be crying by the story's end, but so will you.*

Walter Dean Myers. *Brown Angels.* New York: HarperCollins, 1993.

*Turn-of-the-century photographs of African-American children accompanied by Myers' proudly evocative verse. The book presents a workshop opportunity for parents to bring in photographs that unlock significant memories in their and their children's lives.*

Pat Palmer. *Liking Myself.* San Luis Obispo: Impact Publishers, 1977.

*This is a self-help workbook for children (and parents) that explores the nature and limits of feelings and feeling good. There are a variety of interactive activities and games designed to promote self-esteem and honest communication.*

Gloria Jean Pinkney. *Back Home.* New York: Dial, 1992.

*Eight-year-old Ernestine journeys "back home" to Lumberton, North Carolina. This is a story of belonging, family history, and remarkable eight-year-old independence.*

Faith Ringgold. *Tar Beach.* New York: Crown, 1991.

*"Tar Beach" is the rooftop of the Harlem apartment building where eight-year-old Cassie Louise Lightfoot's dreams of freedom come true. The story is a magical blend of autobiography, fiction, and African-American history. "It's very easy, anyone can fly. All you need is somewhere to go that you can't get to any other way."*

Marjorie Weinman Sharmat. *Gila Monsters Meet You at the Airport.* New York: Penguin, 1983.

*A move from New York City to "out west" serves as a humorous vehicle for examining regional stereotypes and children's fears of moving.*

Chris Van Allsburg. *Two Bad Ants.* Boston: Houghton Mifflin Company, 1988.

*A day in the life of two ants who get lost in the sugar bowl—among other strange and exotic places. The book provides an imaginative and comic focus for discussions about "bad" behavior as well as some interesting math applications once you look closely at the prism shapes of those sugar cubes. Chris Van Allsburg is one of the most "adult" of children's books illustrators, and this book shows how stories can be told as much by their illustrations as by their text.*

Juliet and Charles Snape. *The Boy With Square Eyes.* New York: Simon & Schuster, 1987.

*Charlie watches television all day long and eventually everything "looks square." When his mother notices that even his eyes have become little squares, she unplugs the TV set. The amount of time children spend watching television is of concern to parents, and this "tale of televisionitis" always provokes interesting discussion.*

David Wiesner. *Tuesday.* New York: Houghton Mifflin, 1991.

*We use this book to demonstrate how imaginative and unconventional children's books have become. With its extremely minimal text, the book also shows how story and meaning develop through illustration.*

Audrey Wood. *Elbert's Bad Word.* New York: Harcourt, Brace, Jovanovich, 1988.

*Young Elbert shocks guests at his parents' elegant garden party with a "big, ugly, bad" word. Through the help of a wizard gardener, Elbert learns the difference between "bad" and "strong" words. This book provides a humorous and provocative way of entering into a discussion of discipline issues.*

Taro Yashima. *Crow Boy.* New York: Penguin, 1976.

*This story of a shy boy ostracized by his classmates in a Japanese village school transcends national borders. The gradual awareness of Chibi's individual talents is inspiring and causes readers to reconsider what is truly valued in school.*

Charlotte Zolotow. *This Quiet Lady.* New York: Greenwillow, 1992.

*A young girl explores photographs of her mother as she was growing up. This book lends itself to workshop participants bringing in photographs of their own parents at different stages of their lives.*

read on—the best
endings are beginnings
. . . . . . . . . . . . . . . . . . . . .

*171*

Rosalma Zubizarreta. *La Mujer Que Brillaba Aún Más Que El Sol La Leyenda de Lucía Zenteno.* San Francisco, California: Children's Book Press, 1991.

*Este libro contiene un cuento basado en una leyenda zapoteca, captada por el poeta Mexicano Alejandro Cruz Martínez. Con la intención de rescatar la tradición oral de los indígenas, la escritora y los colaboradores producen un libro bellísimo, describiendo detalladamente como una hermosa mujer, acompañada por miembros del reino animal, y al ser rechazada por su pueblo, en su lindo pelo arrastraba las aguas del río y sus peces.*

## MULTICULTURAL BIBLIOGRAPHY OF CHILDREN'S BOOKS

### AFRICAN AMERICAN

Aardema, V. (1969). *Who's in Rabbit's house?* NY: Dial.

Aardema, V. (1975). *Why mosquitoes buzz in people's ears.* NY: Dial.

Aardema, V. (1981). *Bringing the rain to Kapiti plain.* NY: Dial.

Aardema, V. (1982). *What's so funny, Ketu?* NY: Dial.

Aardema, V. (1983). *Vingananee and the tree toad.* NY: Puffin.

Aardema, V. (1988). *Princess Gorilla and a new kind of water.* NY: Dial.

Adler, D. (1989). *A picture book of Martin Luther King, Jr.* NY: Holiday.

Adoff, A. (1991). *Hard to be six.* NY: Lothrop.

Adoff, A. (1991). *In for spring out for winter.* San Diego: Harcourt Brace Jovanovich.

Albert, B. (1991). *Where does the trail lead?* NY: Simon & Schuster.

Alexander, L. (1992). *The fortune tellers.* NY: Dutton.

Bogart, J.E. (1990). *Daniel's dog.* NY: Scholastic.

Bryan, A. (1989). *Turtle knows your name.* NY: Macmillan.

Bryan, A. (1991). *All night, all day.* NY: Atheneum.

Bryan, A. (1993). *The story of lightning & thunder.* NY: Atheneum.

---

*This multicultural bibliography was prepared by Book Bay, a children's bookstore in Milwaukee, Wisconsin. Reprinted by permission.*

*read on—the best*
*endings are beginnings*
. . . . . . . . . . . . . . . . . . . .

*172*

Bunting, E. (1992). *Summer wheels.* NY: Harcourt Brace.

Cameron, A. (1981). *The stories Julian tells.* NY: Knopf.

Carlstrom, N. (1987). *Wild wild sunflower child.* NY: Macmillan.

Clifton, L. (1992). *Three wishes.* NY: Doubleday.

Collier, J.L. (1991). *Duke Ellington.* NY: Macmillan.

Craft. (1989). *Day of the rainbow.* NY: Viking.

Crewes, D. (1991). *Big mama's.* NY: Greenwillow.

Cummings, P. (1991). *Clean your room Harvey Moon.* NY: Bradbury.

Dee, R. (1991). *Tower to heaven.* NY: Henry Holt.

Dragonwagon, C. (1990). *Half a moon and one whole star.* NY: Macmillan.

Dragonwagon, C. (1990). *Home place.* NY: Macmillan.

Everett, G. (1991). *Li'l Sis and Uncle Willie.* NY: Rizzoli.

Farmer, N. (1993). *Do you know me?* NY: Orchard.

Feelings, M. (1971). *Moja means one.* NY: Dial.

Feelings, M. (1974). *Jambo means hello.* NY: Dial.

Feelings, T. (1978). *Something on my mind.* NY: Dial.

Feelings, T. & E. Greenfield. (1981). *Daydreamers.* NY: Dial.

Golenbock, P. (1990). *Teammates.* San Diego: HBJ.

Gordon, S. (1987). *Waiting for the rain.* NY: Orchard.

Greenfield, E. (1978). *Honey, I love.* NY: Harper.

Greenfield, E. (1988). *Grandpa's face.* NY: Philomel.

Greenfield, E. (1988). *Nathaniel talking.* NY: Black Butterfly.

Greenfield, E. (1988). *Under the Sunday tree.* NY: Harper.

Greenfield, E. (1991). *First pink light.* NY: Black Butterfly.

Greenfield, E. (1991). *Night on Neighborhood Street.* NY: Dial.

Grifalconi, A. (1986). *The village of round and square houses.* Boston: Little, Brown.

Hale, S. (1990). *Mary had a little lamb.* NY: Scholastic.

Haley, G.E. (1970). *A story, a story.* NY: Aladdin.

Hamilton, V. (1985). *The people could fly.* NY: Knopf.

Hamilton, V. (1989). *The bells of Christmas.* San Diego: HBJ.

Hamilton, V. (1990). *Cousins.* NY: Philomel.

Hamilton, V. (1991). *The Al Jahdu storybook.* NY: HBJ.

Hamilton, V. (1993). *Many thousand gone: African Americans from slavery to freedom.* NY: Knopf.

Hart, L. (1991). *How many stars in the sky?* NY: Tambourine.

Havill, J. (1986). *Jamaica's find.* Boston: Houghton Mifflin.

Herlihy, D. (1988). *Ludie's song.* NY: Puffin.

Hill, E. (1990). *Evan's corner.* NY: Viking.

Hoffmann, M. (1991). *Amazing Grace.* NY: Dial.

Hooks, W. (1990). *The ballad of Belle Dorcas.* NY: Knopf.

Hopkinson, D. (1993). *Sweet Clara and the freedom quilt.* NY: Knopf.

Howard, E. (1989). *Chita's Christmas tree.* NY: Bradbury.

Howard, E.F. (1991). *Aunt Flossie's hat (and crabcakes later).* Boston: Clarion.

Isadora, R. (1979). *Ben's trumpet.* NY: Greenwillow.

Isadora, R. (1991). *At the crossroads.* NY: Greenwillow.

Jacobs, S. (1991). *Song of the giraffe.* Boston: Little, Brown.

Johnson, A. (1990). *Do like Kyla.* NY: Orchard.

Johnson, A. (1990). *When I am old with you.* NY: Orchard.

Johnson, A. (1991). *One of three.* NY: Orchard.

Johnson, D. (1991). *What kind of babysitter is this?* NY: Macmillan.

Johnson, J. (1993). *Lift every voice and sing.* NY: Walker.

Jones, R. (1991). *Matthew and Tilly.* NY: Dutton.

Keats, E.J. (1964). *Whistle for Willie.* NY: Penguin.

Keats, E.J. (1965). *John Henry.* NY: Random.

Keats, E.J. (1967). *Peter's chair.* NY: Harper.

Keats, E.J. (1969). *Goggles.* NY: Macmillan.

Kimmel, E. (1988). *Anansi and the moss-covered rock.* NY: Holiday.

*read on—the best*
*endings are beginnings*
. . . . . . . . . . . . . . . . . . . . . .

*174*

Kroll, V. (1992). *Masai and I.* NY: Four Winds.

Kroll, V. (1993). *Africa brothers and sisters.* NY: Four Winds.

Langstaff, J. (1991). *Climbing Jacob's ladder.* NY: Macmillan.

Lawrence, J. (1993). *The great migration.* NY: HarperCollins.

Lewin, H. (1981). *Jafta.* Minneapolis: Carolrhoda.

Lewin, H. (1981). *Jafta and the wedding.* Minneapolis: Carolrhoda.

Lewin, H. (1981). *Jafta's father.* Minneapolis: Carolrhoda.

Lewin, H. (1981). *Jafta's mother.* Minneapolis: Carolrhoda.

Lexau, J.M. (1968). *Striped ice cream.* NY: Scholastic.

Marzollo, J. (1993). *Happy birthday, Martin Luther King.* NY: Scholastic.

Mathis. (1991). *Red dog blue fly.* NY: Viking.

Mattox, C. (1989). *Shake it to the one that you love best.* Nashville: JTG.

McDermott, G. (1992). *Zomo the Rabbit.* NY: Harcourt Brace Jovanovich.

McKissack, P. (1988). *Mirandy and brother wind.* NY: Knopf.

McKissack, P. (1989). *Nettie Jo's friend.* NY: Knopf.

McKissack, P. (1992). *A million fish . . . more or less.* NY: Knopf.

McMillan, B. (1991). *Eating fractions.* NY: Scholastic.

Medearis, S. (1991). *Dancing with the Indians.* NY: Holiday.

Mennes, I. (1990). *Somewhere in Africa.* NY: Dutton.

Mitchell, M. (1993). *Uncle Jed's barbershop.* NY: Simon & Schuster.

Mitchell, R. (1993). *Hue Boy.* NY: Dial.

Mollel, T. (1990). *The orphan boy.* Boston: Clarion.

Mollel, T. (1992). *A promise to the sun.* Boston: Little, Brown.

Musgrove, M. (1976). *Ashanti to Zulu.* NY: Dial.

Myers, W.D. (1988). *Scorpions.* NY: Harper.

Myers, W.D. (1990). *The mouse rap.* NY: Harper.

Myers, W.D. (1992). *Somewhere in the darkness.* NY: Scholastic.

Myers, W.D. (1993). *Brown angels.* NY: HarperCollins.

Naidoo, B. (1986). *Journey to Jo'burg*. NY: Lippincott.

O'Dell, S. (1989). *My name is not Angelica*. NY: Dell.

Parks, R. (1992). *Rosa Parks: My story*. NY: Dial.

Petry, A. (1964). *Tituba of Salem Village*. NY: Harper.

Pinkney, G. (1992). *Back home*. NY: Dial.

Price, L. (1990). *Aida*. San Diego: Harcourt Brace Jovanovich.

Rappaport, D. (1991). *Escape from slavery*. NY: Harper Collins.

Ringgold, F. (1991). *Tar Beach*. NY: Crown.

Robinet, H. (1991). *Children of the fire*. NY: Macmillan.

SanSouci, R. (1989). *The talking eggs*. NY: Dial.

Schermbrucker, R. (1989). *Charlie's house*. NY: Viking.

Schroeder, A. (1990). *Ragtime tumpie*. Boston: Little, Brown.

Serfozo, M. (1990). *Rain talk*. NY: McElderry.

Shine, T.P. (1991). *Make a joyful noise*. NY: Checkerboard.

Slote, A. (1991). *Finding Buck McHenry*. NY: Harper.

Smothers, E. (1992). *Down in the piney woods*. NY: Knopf.

Spinelli, J. (1990). *Maniac Magee*. Boston: Little, Brown.

Steptoe, J. (1980). *Daddy is a monster . . . sometimes*. NY: Lippincott.

Steptoe, J. (1987). *Mofaro's beautiful daughter*. NY: Lothrop.

Stock, C. (1991). *Secret Valentine*. NY: Bradbury.

Sullivan, C. (1991). *Children of promise*. NY: Abrams.

Taylor, M.D. (1989). *Let the circle be unbroken*. NY: Bantam.

Taylor, M.D. (1989). *Roll of thunder, hear my cry*. NY: Bantam.

Taylor, M.D. (1989). *The friendship and the gold cadillac*. NY: Bantam.

Taylor, M.D. (1990). *Mississippi bridge*. NY: Dial.

Taylor, M.D. (1990). *The road to Memphis*. NY: Dial.

Taylor, T. (1970). *The cay*. NY: Avon.

Tusa, T. (1987). *Maebelle's suitcase*. NY: Macmillan.

Udry, J.M. (1991). *What Mary Jo shared*. NY: Scholastic.

*read on—the best*
*endings are beginnings*
. . . . . . . . . . . . . . . . . .

*176*

Walter, M.P. (1980). *Ty's one-man band.* NY: Scholastic.

Walter, M.P. (1991). *Justin and the best biscuits in the world.* NY: Knopf.

Ward, L. (1978). *I am eyes—Nimacho.* NY: Scholastic.

Weir, B. (1991). *Panther dream.* CA: Hyperion.

Williams, K. (1990). *Galimoto.* NY: Lothrop.

Williams, K. (1991). *When Africa was home.* NY: Orchard.

Williams, S. (1992). *Working cotton.* NY: Harcourt Brace Jovanovich.

Williams, V.B. (1984). *Music, music for everyone.* NY: Mulberry.

Williams, V.B. (1986). *Cherries and cherry pits.* NY: Mulberry.

Winter, J. (1988). *Follow the drinking gourd.* NY: Knopf.

Woodson, J. (1990). *Last summer with Maison.* NY: Delacorte.

Woodson, J. (1993). *Between Madison and Palmetto.* NY: Delacorte.

Xiong. (1989). *Nine-in-one, grr! grr!* CA: Children's Book Press.

Yarbrough, C. (1979). *Cornrows.* NY: Coward-McCann.

Yarbrough, C. (1990). *The shimmershine queens.* NY: Knopf.

## NATIVE AMERICAN

Bierhorst, J. (1984). *Spirit child.* NY: Morrow.

Cohlene, T. (1990). *Dancing drum.* Mahwah, NJ: Watermill Press.

Cohlene, T. (1990). *Ka-ha-si and the lion.* Mahwah, NJ: Watermill Press.

Cohlene, T. (1990). *Quillworker.* Mahwah, NJ: Watermill Press.

Cohlene, T. (1990). *Turquoise boy.* Mahwah, NJ: Watermill Press.

de Paola, T. (1983). *The legend of the bluebonnet.* NY: Putnam.

de Paola, T. (1988). *The legend of the Indian paintbrush.* NY: Putnam.

Esbensen, B. (1989). *Ladder to the sky.* Boston: Little, Brown.

Goble, P. (1978). *The girl who loved wild horses.* NY: Aladdin.

Goble, P. (1980). *The gift of the sacred dog.* NY: Aladdin.

Goble, P. (1984). *Buffalo woman.* NY: Aladdin.

Goble, P. (1989). *Beyond the ridge.* NY: Bradbury.

Goble, P. (1991). *The great race.* NY: Aladdin.

Grossmant, V. & Long, S. (1991). *Ten little rabbits.* San Francisco: Chronicle.

Highwater, J. (1977). *Anpao.* NY: Harper.

Hobbs, S.W. (1989). *Bearstone.* NY: Avon.

Hobbs, S.W. (1993). *Beardance.* NY: Atheneum.

Holling, C. (1969). *Paddle to the sea.* Boston: Houghton Mifflin.

Hotze, S. (1988). *A circle unbroken.* NY: Houghton Mifflin.

Hudson, J. (1984). *Sweetgrass.* NY: Scholastic.

Hudson, J. (1990). *Dawn rider.* NY: Scholastic.

Jeffers, S. (1991). *Brother Eagle, Sister Sky.* NY: Dial.

Link/Blood. (1976). *The goat in the rug.* NY: Macmillan.

Locker, T. (1991). *Land of the gray wolf.* NY: Dial.

Mayo, G. (1987). *Star tales.* NY: Walker.

Mayo, G. (1989). *Earthmakers tale.* NY: Walker.

Mayo, G. (1993). *Meet Tricky Coyote.* NY: Walker.

McDermott, G. (1974). *Arrow to the sun.* NY: Puffin.

Medearis, S. (1991). *Dancing with the Indians.* NY: Holiday.

Naylor, P. (1973). *To walk the sky path.* NY: Dell.

O'Dell, S. (1986). *Streams to the river, river to the sea.* NY: Houghton Mifflin.

O'Dell, S. (1992). *Thunder rolling in the mountains.* Boston: Houghton Mifflin.

Osofsky, A. (1992). *Dreamcatcher.* NY: Orchard.

Paulsen, G. (1990). *Canyons.* NY: Delacorte.

Pitts, P. (1988). *Racing the sun.* NY: Avon.

Riordan, J. (1984). *The woman in the moon.* NY: Dial.

Roop, C. (1992). *Ahyoka and the talking leaves.* NY: Lothrop.

Shannon, M. (1992). *The rough-faced girl.* NY: Putnam.

Sneve, V.D.H. (1989). *Dancing teepees.* NY: Holiday House.

Van Laan, N. (1989). *Rainbow crow.* NY: Knopf.

Yellow Rose, R. (1979). *Tonweya and the eagle.* NY: Penguin.

Yolen, J. (1990). *Sky Dogs.* San Diego: Harcourt Brace Jovanovich

Yolen, J. (1992). *Encounter.* NY: Harcourt Brace.

## *HISPANIC*

Aardema, V. (1991). *Borreguita and the coyote.* NY: Knopf.

Adler, D. (1993). *Picture book of Simon Boliver.* NY: Holiday.

Beatty, P. (1981). *Lupita Manana.* NY: Morrow.

Buss, F. (1991). *Journey of the sparrows.* NY: Dutton.

Carlson, L.M., ed. (1990). *Where angels glide at dawn: New stories from Latin America.* NY: Harper.

Delacre. (1989). *Arroz con leche.* NY: Scholastic.

Dorros, A. (1991). *Abuela.* NY: Dutton.

Gallo, D. (1993). *Join in multiethnic short stories.* NY: Delacorte.

George, J.C. (1989). *Shark beneath the reef.* NY: Harper.

Paulsen, G. (1987). *The crossing.* NY: Orchard.

Roe, E. (1991). *With my brother/Con mi hermano.* NY: Bradbury.

Staples, S. (1993). *Haveli.* NY: Knopf.

Trevino, E. (1989). *El Guero.* NY: HarperCollins.

Vidal, B. (1991). *The legend of El Dorado.* NY: Knopf.

Winter, J. (1991). *Diego.* NY: Knopf.

## *ASIAN AMERICAN*

Choi, S. (1993). *Echoes of the white giraffe.* NY: Houghton Mifflin.

Coerr, E. (1993). *Mieko and the fifth treasure.* NY: Putnam.

Compton, P. (1991). *The terrible eek.* NY: Simon & Schuster.

Demi. (1990). *The empty pot.* NY: Holt.

Demi. (1991). *Chingis Khan.* NY: Holt.

Friedman, I.R. (1984). *How my parents learned to eat.* Boston: Houghton Mifflin.

Garland, S. (1993). *Lotus seed.* NY: Harcourt Brace Jovanovich.

*read on—the best
endings are beginnings*
. . . . . . . . . . . . . . . . . . . . . .

*179*

Gerstein, M. (1987). *The mountains of Tibet.* NY: Harper.

Hong, L.T. (1990). *How the ox star fell from heaven.* Whitman.

Kimmel, E. (1991). *The greatest of all.* NY: Holiday House.

Lee, J.M. (1982). *Legend of the milky way.* NY: Holt.

Lee, J.M. (1985). *Toad is the uncle of heaven.* NY: Holt.

Lee, J.M. (1991). *Silent lotus.* NY: Farrar.

Lee, M. (1993). *If it hadn't been for Yoon Jun.* NY: Houghton Mifflin.

Levine, A. (1993). *Boy who drew cats.* NY: Dial.

Levitin, S. (1993). *The golem and the dragon girl.* NY: Dial.

Lobel, A. (1982). *Ming Lo moves the mountain.* NY: Scholastic.

Louie, A.L. (1982). *Yeh-Shen.* NY: Philomel.

Mosel, A. (1972). *The funny little woman.* NY: Dutton.

Nomura, R. (1991). *Grandpa's town.* Brooklyn: Kane/Miller.

Parker, R.A. (1990). *Grandfather Tang's story.* NY: Crown.

Pellegrini, N. (1991). *Families are different.* NY: Holiday House.

Pinkwater, D. (1975). *Wingman.* NY: Bantam.

Pittman, H. (1986). *A grain of rice.* NY: Bantam.

Rappaport, D. (1991). *The journey of Meng.* NY: Dial.

Say, A. (1993). *Grandfather's journey.* Boston: Houghton Mifflin.

Surat, M. (1983). *Angel child, dragon child.* NY: Scholastic.

Tompert, A. (1993). *Bamboo hats and a rice cake.* NY: Crown.

Tsutsui, Y. (1983). *Anna's special present.* NY: Puffin.

Vuong, L. (1982). *The brocaded slipper & other Vietnamese tales.* NY: HarperCollins.

Vuong, L. (1993). *Sky legends of Vietnam.* NY: HarperCollins.

Whelan, G. (1992). *Goodby Vietnam.* NY: Bantam.

Willis, R. (1992). *A to Zen: A book of Japanese culture.* NY: Simon & Schuster.

Yep, L. (1977). *Child of the owl.* NY: Harper.

Yep, L. (1989). *The rainbow people.* NY: Harper.

*read on—the best
endings are beginnings*
. . . . . . . . . . . . . . . . . . . . . . .
*180*

Yep, L. (1991). *The star fisher.* NY: Morrow.

Yep, L. (1991). *Tongues of jade.* NY: Harper.

Young, E. (1989). *Lon Po Po.* NY: Philomel.

## OTHER

Aardema, V. (1991). *Traveling to Tondo.* NY: Knopf.

AnneVolkmer, J. (1990). *Song of the charimia.* Minneapolis: Carolrhoda.

Baer, E. (1990). *This is the way we go to school.* NY: Scholastic.

Dorros, A. (1990). *Rain forest secret.* NY: Scholastic.

Fischetto, L. (1991). *The jungle is my home.* NY: Viking.

George, J.C. (1972). *Julie of the wolves.* NY: Harper.

Gray, N. (1988). *A country far away.* NY: Orchard.

Heide, F. (1992). *Sami and the time of the troubles.* NY: Houghton Mifflin.

Heide, F. & Gilliland, J. (1990). *The day of Ahmed's secret.* NY: Lothrop.

Hill, E. (1967). *Evan's corner.* NY: Viking.

Ichikawa, S. (1985). *Here a little child I stand.* NY: Philomel.

Joosse, B. (1991). *Mama, do you love me?* San Francisco: Chronicle.

Kimmel, E. (1991). *Baba Yaga.* NY: Holiday House.

Kimmel, E. (1991). *Bearhead.* NY: Holiday House.

Kuskin, K. (1987). *Jerusalem shining still.* NY: Harper.

Lankford, M. (1992). *Hopscotch around the world.* NY: Morrow.

Levitin, S. (1987). *The return.* NY: Fawcett Juniper.

Markun, P. (1993). *The little painter of Sabana Grande.* NY: Bradbury.

Martin, B. (1987). *Here are my hands.* NY: Holt.

Morris, A. (1989). *Bread, bread, bread.* NY: Lothrop.

Morris, A. (1990). *Loving.* NY: Lothrop.

O'Dell, S. (1987). *Island of the blue dolphins.* NY: Dell Yearling.

O'Dell, S. (1988). *Black star, bright dawn.* NY: Houghton Mifflin.

Oppenheim, S. (1992). *The lily cupboard.* NY: Harper.

Paterson, K. (1990). *The tale of the mandarin ducks.* NY: Lodestar.

Pinkwater, J. (1991). *Tails of the Bronx*. NY: Macmillan.

Polacco, P. (1990). *Just plain fancy*. NY: Bantam.

Polacco, P. (1992). *Mrs. Katz and Tush*. NY: Bantam.

Rosen, B. (1991). *Andi's war*. NY: Puffin.

Rosen, M. (1992). *How the animals got their colors*. NY: Harcourt Brace.

Sacks, M. (1989). *Beyond safe boundaries*. NY: Dutton.

Shannon, G. (1990). *More stories to solve*. NY: Greenwillow.

Shetterly, S. (1990). *The dwarf-wizard of Uxmal*. NY: Atheneum.

Singer, M. (1991). *Nine o'clock lullaby*. NY: Harper.

Spier, P. (1980). *People*. NY: Doubleday.

Stanley, F. (1991). *The last princess*. NY: Macmillan.

Staples, S. (1989). *Shabanu: Daughter of the wind*. NY: Knopf.

Steiner, B. (1988). *Whale brother*. NY: Walker.

Taylor, T. (1993). *Timothy of the cay*. NY: Harcourt Brace.

Williams, V.B. (1990). *More, more, more, said the baby*. NY: Greenwillow.

Winter, J. (1992). *Klara's new world*. NY: Knopf.

Yolen, J. (1992). *Street rhymes around the world*. NY: St. Martin's Press.

## PARENT RESOURCES

## BOOKS AND BROCHURES

*Guide to Parent Involvement Resources*. National Committee for Citizens in Education, 900 2nd Street, N.E., Suite 8, Washington, DC 20002-3557, 202-408-0447.

*"Parent Resources" bibliography is reprinted from Vol. 7, Number 3, Rethinking Schools, 1001 E. Keefe Ave., Milwaukee, WI 53212. 414-964-9646*

*A production of the Council of Chief State School Officers and the National Coalition for Parent Involvement in Education, the guide outlines the activities and publications of over 30 national organizations working for parent involvement in schools.*

*First Teachers: Parental Involvement in the Public Schools.* National School Boards Association, P.O. Box 63422, Baltimore, MD 21263-0422. $15.00 plus $3.75 shipping and handling, pre-paid.

*Designed to help school board members understand the issues surrounding parental involvement, including the benefits of involvement, the educational, societal, and demographic barriers that can discourage participation, and policy implications for school boards. The booklet also includes descriptions of model programs from around the country.*

*Beyond the Bake Sale: An Educators' Guide to Working with Parents,* by Anne T. Henderson, Carl L. Marburger, and Theodora Ooms. National Committee for Citizens in Education, 900 2nd Street, N.E., Suite 8, Washington, DC 20002-3557, 202-408-0447. $10.95 plus $2.50 postage and handling.

*Encourages teachers and administrators to look critically at their beliefs and feelings about parental involvement. Practical advice on how to make parents feel more welcome and foster a collaborative atmosphere among parents and school staff.*

*The Little Things Make a Big Difference: How to Help Your Children Succeed in School.* National Association of Elementary School Principals. Send a self-addressed, stamped business-sized envelope to Station 9/NAESP, 101 Northwest Point Boulevard, Elk Grove Village, IL 60007-1019.

*A free 17-page booklet for parents based on suggestions from a survey of 10,000 elementary and middle school principals. Outlines concrete steps parents can take to help ensure their children's enjoyment and success in learning.*

*101 Ways Parents Can Help Students Achieve.* American Association of School Administrators, 1801 N. Moore Street, Arlington, VA 22209-9988, 703-528-0700. $6.00 pre-paid; bulk prices available.

*Specific ideas to enrich childhood education every day. Topics include learning at home, using the newspaper, building self-esteem, parent involvement in the school, and others.*

*read on—the best
endings are beginnings*
. . . . . . . . . . . . . . . . . . . . . . .

*183*

*Parents, Schools, and the Law*, by David Schimmel and Louis Fischer. National Committee for Citizens in Education, 900 2nd Street, N.E., Suite 8, Washington, DC 20002-3557, 202-408-0447. $10.95 plus $2.50 shipping and handling.

*A guide for parents that is free of unnecessary legal jargon and offers vital information on the law as it concerns schools and discrimination, freedom of religion, discipline, freedom of expression, testing, and other topics. The appendices summarize relevant court decisions and constitutional amendments.*

*Beyond the Open Door*, by Nancy Berla and Susan Hlesciak Hall. National Committee for Citizens in Education, 900 2nd Street, N.E., Suite 8, Washington, DC 20002-3557, 202-408-0447. $10.00 plus $2.50 postage and handling.

*Reference guide to regulations regarding school board meetings in the 50 states and D.C. Useful for parents and citizens interested in increasing public access to local school board meetings and school board accountability.*

*Information for Parents*. National Committee for Citizens in Education, 900 2nd Street, N.E., Suite 8, Washington, DC 20002-3557, 202-408-0447. $4.95 for the set, plus $2.50 shipping and handling.

*A series of twelve brochures for parents. Each brochure contains concise information on a single topic including parent organizing, student discipline, access to records, student rights, and dropout prevention. Also available in Spanish.*

*A Handbook for Immigrant Parents: Protect the Educational Rights of Your Children*. META, Inc., 524 Union Street, San Francisco, CA 94133, 415-398-1997. $2.00.

*A guide to help foreign-born parents understand their rights regarding their children's education in the U.S. The handbook, which is available in Spanish and English, gives special consideration to parents' concerns about immigration authorities' access to the family's school records and related information.*

*Together Is Better: Building Strong Partnerships Between Schools and Hispanic Parents*. Hispanic Policy Development Project, 1001 Connecticut Ave., N.W., Suite 538, Washington, DC 20036, 202-822-8414. $9.00 (including UPS fee).

*read on—the best
endings are beginnings*
. . . . . . . . . . . . . . . . . . . .

184

*Strategies and techniques for teachers, principals, and school districts,
derived from 42 HPDP-funded parent/school partnership projects designed
to encourage cooperation between Hispanic parents and their children's
schools.*

*You're a Parent . . . You're a Teacher Too* and *Queridos Padres: En los Esta-
dos Unidos la escuela es nuestra tambien.* Hispanic Policy Development
Project, 1001 Connecticut Ave., N.W., Suite 538, Washington, DC
20036, 202-822-8414. $.50 each (including postage and handling); ask
about bulk prices.

*Separate English and Spanish versions of a message to U.S. Hispanic par-
ents explaining why parents are important in the education of their children
and how they can work with the schools their children attend.*

*Helping Dreams Survive: The Story of a Project Involving African-Ameri-
can Families in the Education of Their Children,* by Jocelyn A. Garling-
ton. National Committee for Citizens in Education, 900 2nd Street,
N.E., Suite 8, Washington, DC 20002-3557, 202-408-0447. $24.95 plus
$2.50 shipping and handling.

*Book documenting the "With and For Parents" project in Baltimore, Md.,
provides an inspiring yet realistic look at an urban parent and family
involvement effort. The program, which ran from 1987 to 1990, was
designed to help low-income minority parents encourage their children to
stay in school and graduate.*

*What the Outgoing PA President Should Have Told the Incoming PA Presi-
dent.* Community Resource Exchange, 17 Murray Street, 5th Floor,
New York, NY 10007, 212-349-8155. $10.00 for parents ($25.00 for
others).

*A useful resource for new PA or PTA leadership on fundraising, member-
ship development, by-laws, negotiations, and relationships with teachers
and administrators. Loose-leaf for easy photocopying. A glossary is
included.*

*The Evidence Continues to Grow: Parent Involvement Improves Student
Achievement,* edited by Anne T. Henderson. National Committee for
Citizens in Education, 900 2nd Street, N.E., Suite 8, Washington, DC
20002-3557, 202-408-0447. $10.00 plus $2.50 shipping and handling.

*A detailed annotated bibliography of 49 studies showing how parents'
involvement improves their children's performance in school, from pre-
school to high school. The studies described build an excellent case for
increased parental involvement.*

*read on—the best
endings are beginnings*
. . . . . . . . . . . . . . . . . . . . . .

*185*

*Organizing for Better School Food.* Center for Science in the Public Interest, 1875 Connecticut Avenue, N.W., Suite 300, Washington, D.C. 20009-5728. $7.00.

*A 42-page booklet which is an excellent place to start a school food improvement effort. Encourages activists to review school food as critically as we do other "educational support materials." Provides clear methods for action, including coalition building, media techniques, and background on federal law and food service contracts. Includes a collection of success stories with activists to contact and a list of resources.*

*Crossing the Tracks: How "Untracking" Can Save America's Schools,* by Anne Wheelock. The New Press, 450 W. 41st St., 6th Floor, New York, NY 10036. $19.95.

*A critical look at tracking with an emphasis on groups around the country that are successfully organizing against tracking in their area schools. Includes a state-by-state list of schools that are eliminating ability grouping.*

*Maintaining Inequality: A Background Packet on Tracking and Ability Grouping.* National Coalition of Education Activists, P.O. Box 405, Rosendale, NY 12472, 914-658-8115. $3.00; bulk prices available.

*Includes basic information on what tracking is and how its use affects children, articles by parents and anti-tracking activists, sample resolutions, and more.*

*Keeping Track: How Schools Structure Inequality,* by Jeannie Oakes. Yale University Press, New Haven, CT. 1985.

*A classic work on how tracking hurts slower and average students and fails to significantly benefit advanced students, and how the practice influences every aspect of school experience.*

*Standardized Tests and Our Children: A Guide to Testing Reform.* Fair Test, 342 Broadway, Cambridge, MA 02139, 617-864-4810. $4.00; ask about bulk prices.

*A 32-page booklet explaining what standardized tests are, how they are used and misused, and why their use is a detriment to education. Gives recommendations on strategy for testing reform activists. Also available in Spanish.*

*Standing Up to the SAT.* FairTest, 342 Broadway, Cambridge, MA 02139, 617-864-4810. $6.95.

*For high school students taking the SAT, this book can be a useful tool for improving scores. It also looks at the many ways the SAT and other standard admission tests discriminate against students on the basis of race, ethnicity, language, sex, and income, and offers ways to fight the overuse and misuse of the tests.*

*None of the Above: Behind the Myth of Scholastic Aptitude,* by David Owen.

*A highly recommended but out-of-print book which exposes the SAT for the unreliable, big-business enterprise that it is. Check local libraries for copies.*

*False Choices: Why School Vouchers Threaten Our Children's Future.* A special issue of *Rethinking Schools*. 1001 E. Keefe Ave., Milwaukee, WI 53212, 414-964-9646. $3.00 plus $2.00 shipping and handling.

*A unique resource examining the danger school choice and voucher plans pose to public schools and America's democratic vision. Includes articles by Jonathan Kozol, Deborah Meier, Herb Kohl, and Maxine Waters.*

## ORGANIZATIONS

National Committee for Citizens in Education, 900 2nd St., N.E., Suite 8, Washington, DC 20002-3557, 202-408-0447.

*National organization to expand parents and other citizens' access to public schools and build coalitions for public school reform. Publishes numerous high-quality resources, including a newsletter, pocket guides, brochures, and books on parent's rights, school-based reform, and parent involvement. Also runs two hotlines for questions concerning citizen involvement in schools: 1-800-NETWORK (English) and 1-800-LE-AYUDA (Spanish).*

National Association for the Education of Young Children, 1834 Connecticut Avenue., N.W., Washington, DC., 20009-5786, 800-424-2460.

*Catalogue offers books, videos, brochures, posters, and tapes for teachers and parents of children from birth to eight years old. Topics covered include achievement testing, safety, media violence, discipline, school readiness, and many others.*

National Parent and Teacher Association, 700 N. Rush St., Chicago, IL 60611-2571, 312-787-0977.

*Provides information to parents and Parent and Teacher Associations on building home-school relationships, developing parenting skills, improving learning at home, and promoting parent-child communication. Single copies of many resources are free and some are available in Spanish.*

The Parent Institute, P.O. Box 7474, Fairfax Station, VA 22039, 800-756-5525.

*Produces two newsletters for school staff and parents which are published during the school year. Also offers inexpensive booklets for parents on how they can help their children learn to read, build self-esteem, encourage responsible behavior and motivation, and improve communication.*

The Right Question Project, 167 Holland St., Somerville, MA 02144, 617-628-4070.

*A training program that teaches parents to advocate on behalf of their children and schools. Using role play and discussion, teaches parents to ask questions of school and public officials, to think critically about their children's schooling, and to hold public institutions accountable.*

Multicultural Education Training and Advocacy (META, Inc.), 524 Union Street, San Francisco, CA 94133, 415-398-1997.

*An advocacy organization which works for the full participation of poor children in education. Focusing on immigrant and linguistic minority students, META provides counseling and training to parents and activists, organizes parents into multiethnic coalitions for change, and litigates on behalf of poor and minority students' rights.*

Clearinghouse for Immigrant Education (CHIME), 1-800-441-7192, c/o National Coalition of Advocates for Students, 100 Boylston Street, Suite 737, Boston, MA 02116.

*Offers parents, teachers, and students information on legal rights, bilingual education, student support services, multicultural education, and other topics. Some material is available in foreign language editions.*

ASPIRA Association, Inc., 1112 16th St., N.W., #340, Washington, DC 20036, 202-835-3600.

*Aids Latino youth and their families in decreasing dropout rates, developing mentoring programs, and increasing Hispanic parent involvement in schools. Publishes a quarterly newsletter and other materials.*

National Urban League, Inc., 500 E. 62nd St., New York, NY 10021, 212-310-9214.

*Through its network of 113 affiliates around the country, provides parents with training to help parents assist their children with homework and math and science activities, and provides counseling about college admissions and financial aid.*

*read on—the best
endings are beginnings*
. . . . . . . . . . . . . . . . . . . .

*188*

Coalition for Quality Education, 1702 Upton Ave., Toledo, OH 43607, 419-537-9246.

*Founded in 1978, this grass-roots organization conducts workshops and training for parents, monitors policies and practices of the Toledo Public Schools, takes legal action when necessary, and works with elected officials on reform. Has brochures on standardized testing and school discipline issues.*

Books Project, c/o Network of Educators on the Americas, 1118 22nd St., N.W., Washington, DC 20037, 202-429-0137.

*Coordinates the Family Involvement Project, a parent and student writing program in which participants write brief stories or essays about their lives and share them with each other. The project is designed to increase parents' comfort in the school environment, promote literacy, and foster understanding between parents and school staff.*

League of Schools Reaching Out, a project of the Institute for Responsive Education, 605 Commonwealth Ave., Boston, MA 02215, 617-353-3309.

*Works with member schools to get parents and families involved in identifying and addressing problems that face schools and the children they serve. The League has 75 member schools around the country working on a wide variety of projects.*

The Center for Law and Education, 955 Massachusetts Ave., Cambridge, MA, 02139, 617-876-6611.

*Assists parents in advocating on behalf of their communities for quality public education. Provides referrals to local legal services and education advocacy groups. Most publications are intended for legal advocates, but some materials might be useful to parents. Write or call for publications list.*

People for the American Way, 2000 M St., N.W., Suite 400, Washington, DC 20036, 202-467-4999.

*Promotes anti-censorship efforts. Publishes* Attacks on the Freedom to Learn, *a yearly state-by-state survey of censorship attempts in the schools.*

FairTest (National Center for Fair and Open Testing), 342 Broadway, Cambridge, MA 02139, 617-864-4810.

*Campaigns for elimination or reform of standardized testing at all levels of education. Provides activists with materials for organizing testing reform efforts in their communities and publishes several resources on standardized testing and its detrimental effects on education and students.*

Parents and Teachers Against Violence in Education (PTAVE), P.O. Box 1033, Alamo, CA 94507-7033, 510-831-1611.

*Publishes materials against corporal punishment in schools. Some materials are available in Spanish.*

People Opposed to Paddling Students (POPS), P.O. Box 19045, Houston, TX 77224, 713-493-6232.

*Activist organization which works for the abolition of corporal punishment in schools. Publishes a quarterly newsletter for members and school and elected officials.*

# Works Cited

Daniels, Harvey and Steven Zemelman. 1985. *A Writing Project.* Portsmouth, NH: Heinemann.

Graves, Donald. 1983. *Writing: Teachers & Children at Work.* Portsmouth, NH: Heinemann.

Lyons, Bill. March 1981. "The PQP Method of Responding to Writing." *English Journal,* 70–71.

Progoff, Ira. 1975. *At a Journal Workshop.* New York: Dialogue House.

Reid, Sally and R. Craig Sautter. 1991. *An Evaluation of Parent Involvement Projects.* Chicago: The Joyce Foundation.

Rief, Linda. 1992. *Seeking Diversity.* Portsmouth, NH: Heinemann.

Sautter: R. Craig. 1991. Interviews of Parent Project participants conducted for The Joyce Foundation.